TRIAL TAPPERS

TAPPING LIFE'S TRIALS TO PRODUCE POSITIVE GROWTH

12 Tools to Survive Trials from Health and Finance or Traumas from Sex Abuse to Suicide

Hugh D. Watt

© 2020 Hugh D. Watt

All rights reserved. No portion of this book may be reproduced, stored in a retrieval system, or transmitted in any form or by any means—electronic, mechanical, photocopy, recording, scanning, or other—except for brief quotations in critical reviews or articles, without the prior written permission of the publisher.

- Some names and identifying details have been changed to protect the privacy of individuals.
- I have tried to recreate events, locales and conversations from my memories of them. In order to maintain their anonymity in some instances I have changed the names of individuals and places, I may have changed some identifying characteristics and details such as physical properties, occupations and places of residence.
- Although the author and publisher have made every effort to ensure that the information in this book was correct at press time, the author and publisher do not assume and hereby disclaim any liability to any party for any loss, damage, or disruption caused by errors or omissions, whether such errors or omissions result from negligence, accident, or any other cause.
- This book is not intended as a substitute for the medical advice of physicians. The reader should regularly consult a physician in matters relating to his/her health and particularly with respect to any symptoms that may require diagnosis or medical attention.
- Proper names used in this book have been done so with their permission and stories or examples related to each have been approved prior to publishing. Some names have been changed to protect identities.

Published in 2020
ISBN 978-1-7432791-1-5 (paperback)
ISBN 978-1-7342791-3-9 (ePub)
Library of Congress Copyright 2020, Registration Number TX008861312 / 2020-03-17
Cover Design by: Manshuri Yusuf
Illustrations by: Tanveer Khan
Cover Photography by: Luc Brousseau/shutterstock.com
Book Layout © 2017 BookDesignTemplates.com

Dedication

Dedicated to my parents, my wife, my children, grandchildren, brothers, and sister.

Endorsements

During the past decade, I've gotten to know Hugh Watt as both the consummate professional he is, as well as the incredible human being behind this book. Hugh Watt is 100 percent trustworthy, he's 100 percent honest, and he rates a 100 percent at caring and compassion towards those fortunate enough to have been his clients, and now, those equally fortunate to come across *Trial Tappers*! Everyone can benefit from this rare display of openness and the life lessons learned along the way. Readers will gain a greater and greater sense of curiosity as they delve into its pages. Hugh Watt is indeed a master story-teller! He had me at "My brother Cody was only 29 years old when he decided his trials in life were . . ." And I don't believe I felt this way just because I'd found my mother in an attempt to take her life, and thus identified somewhat with Hugh's gripping account. I resonated with this opening because as it moved along, I felt an anticipation to learn the entire story! That's Hugh's gift—on display and available to bless lives! I'm hoping Hugh Watt and his vital message can reach a vast and grateful readership!

Brad Anderson
Co-founder Covey Leadership Center.
Produced *The Seven Habits of Highly Effective People*.
Author: *The View from Under My Desk–My Battle with Depression in the Workplace*
Beacon Publishing Group

ENDORSEMENTS

While the area of Post-Traumatic Growth has been with us now for several decades, Hugh Watt gives us a new creative and practical path to pursue that can enable the reader to move beyond the effects of trauma. More importantly, in highlighting the reality of positive growth beyond trauma, Hugh takes us on this journey from the perspective not, only of a practitioner, but also as a survivor. For those who are searching for renewal after the trauma, *Trial Tappers* is a must read.

Mark J. Maggio, Ph.D.
Chairman of the Board, Emeritus
International Critical Incident Stress Foundation

I have had the privilege of knowing the author for over 20 years. I was so pleased when he decided to write a book that addresses such important issues. I respect that he is so authentic in his approach, especially in regards to his own experiences, and does not shy away from tough topics. Further, I appreciate that along with addressing the arena of traumas, he gives specific tools that when followed leads the reader on a path that can, through putting in the work, result in healing. As a clinician, I would highly recommend this book to those I serve. I believe it encourages behaviors that, frankly, begin at the beginning. Further as a clinician, I recommend this book to my colleagues. The work we do impacts us in a variety of ways. I believe this book can help us too as we navigate the narrative of others.

Dr. Ruth Gerritsen-McKane, LCSW

ENDORSEMENTS

I found this book helpful because it puts in simple words what are complex and difficult experiences. This allows me to make sense of overwhelming events and take action to get through the emotions that are interfering with daily life. Now, I can start thinking about my experiences in a meaningful way, take action, take charge, and feel much more in control of my life. I can also teach this material to others and help them make it through traumatic events that are inevitable, at one time or another, in all of our lives.

Walter T. Simon, Ph.D.
President-Progressive Therapy Systems

We all go through trials in life. Trials can make us bitter or better. The book *Trial Tappers* helps us understand and apply the principles to make us better. Hugh has gone through his own trials in life, including sexual trauma, and has become a better person because of the principles he has incorporated into his life. He is speaking from experience. I honor him for being so open about his past. He teaches us how to become a Trial Tapper by recognizing the answers and growth come from within. We can all learn from this book and tap into ourselves to grow from the trials in our lives. Our trials don't need to paralyze us. Hugh says, "Grief is the reality of trials in life, yet empowerment is the result of a life of grief." To all who struggle, I would recommend you read this book. I hope that you can find the path that comes from pain that will help you grow.

Jason Webb MSW, LCSW
Author: *The Reality of Perception*

ENDORSEMENTS

Reading *Trial Tappers* made me reflect on many of the incidents that I have been involved in throughout my life, both personally and professionally. After having spent 37 years in law enforcement, I have seen and experienced many situations that have left a lasting impact on me. As I put those experiences through the perspective of the various taps, it allowed me to see them through different lenses, ones which showed me, not only the growth I had experienced as a result of the experience, but also some that I had not come through as cleanly as I may have thought I had.

Using the Trial Action Path (TAP) approach Hugh teaches, the reader is able to understand the "normalcy" of their experience, but more importantly the ability to work through it and the potential to come out the other end a better and stronger person because of it. Simple, straightforward steps are what many need to work through their experiences, free from the psychobabble that shuts down many from following through with their care. Though simple and straightforward, it is not a quick fix to what ails us, but rather a set of steps that, when a person is ready to take that step, will guide them toward healing and growth.

Geoffrey Leggett,
Assistant Chief of Police

Contents

Preface i

SECTION I FOUNDATION 1

    Foundation 3

SECTION II SAFETY & GROUND SUPPORTS 29

    TAP #1: Tap Your Life's Trials – We ALL Have Pain!............... 31

    TAP #2: Tap Your Season of Symptoms – S.O.S. 51

    TAP #3: Tap Your Helpful Others – Family OR Friends! 83

    TAP #4: Tap Your Unseen Power to Overcome Trials – Bigger than Yourself! 105

    TAP #5: Tap Your Supports during Unexpected Storms – Prepare for the Worst! 115

SECTION III RESILIENCE & EDUCATION 125

    TAP #6: Tap Your Protective Vest – Balanced Life Helps! 127

    TAP #7: Tap Your Yoyo Grief Cycle – Reality of Grief! 137

    TAP #8: Tap Your Pit of Despair – Start Climbing, Get Out! 149

    TAP #9: Tap Your Trauma Trash Can – Empty the Hidden Trauma! 157

SECTION IV STRENGTHS & EMPOWERMENT 173

    TAP #10: Tap Your Outside Resistance – Get Motivated! 175

CONTENTS

TAP #11: Tap Your Hammer – Channel the Pain! 185

TAP #12: Tap Your Inner Fire – The Long Process Works! ... 197

Summary 207

References and Works Cited 223

Would You Provide a Testimonial? 225

Acknowledgements

Influential People

It is obvious that I have had many influential people helping me in my life. I have a chapter called Tap Helpful Others. The following people have helped me, directly or indirectly, by their methods of teaching. Note that it is impossible to list everyone.

Apple Valley High School instructors: Mr. Brimhall, Mr. Lento, Mr. and Ms. Leary, Mr. Walton, Ms. Moore, Mr. Eaton, Mr. Kurtz, Mr. Sauers and Juanita Chow.

Formal Education instructors: Brent A. Barlow, George and Diane Pace, Truman and Ann Madsen, Nafez Nazzal, Rabbi David Rosen, Dr. Walter T. Simon, and Morri Namaste and books by the following authors: The Arbinger Institute, Stephen R. Covey, Viktor Frankl, John Gray, Robert Kiyosaki, Harve Eker, Russell Brunson and the Why Try Organization.

I have gained so much strength and knowledge from relationships with personal examples of turning trials into strengths. These are my closest friends, master instructors, authors, and friends: Jason Webb, Dave Murray, Christian Moore, Rick Delray, Hugh Ebmeyer, Bruce Ebmeyer, Sean Core, Dan Redando, Brad Anderson, Greg Hendrix, Greg Petersen, John L. Warner, Brian Blevins, Bob and Robbi Ann Sorensen, Hunter Finch, and Ruth Gerritsen-McKane, Heather Severn Callister to name a few.

ACKNOWLEDGEMENTS

Visual Graphics Acknowledgment

Special thanks to **Tanveer Khan** for helping make my imagination come to life in visual art and graphics for others to follow my visual stories to navigate our trials in life.

Feedback Acknowledgment

Special thanks to Georgia Cordle, Lisa Glade, Ruth Gerritsen-McKane, Jason Webb, and Dino and Shannon Watt for taking the time to read this book in draft form and to provide valuable feedback.

Editing Acknowledgment

Special thanks to Janet Olcott for taking the time to edit this book. There are no words to express how grateful I am for the many hours she has spent with me editing this book.

Also thanks to Georgia Cordle and Becky Tilton for taking time to provide valuable feedback and additional edits.

Preface

My brother Cody was only twenty-nine years old when he decided his trials in life were too difficult to handle. The pain and anguish of his suicide was a trial almost more than I could handle. I mourned for his two daughters, our siblings, his adopted parents, and myself. Cody had chosen not to have contact with most of his family over his last few years, and his passing left me struggling with the loss on a very deep level. I had to rely heavily on my fifty years' worth of life experiences, training, family support, and knowledge to help me get through the weeks that followed that awful day. As the oldest son, I was responsible to help my mother prepare for the funeral and the arrival and gathering of family and friends. Over the last week I hadn't slept much and was emotionally drained on the day of the funeral. If you have experienced the death of a loved one, you know too well the emotional state I was in.

The big problem for me was, as the oldest brother and a professional therapist who specialized in mental health and substance abuse, I had been unable to convince my own brother that there was help. I had been a licensed clinical therapist for more than twenty years. I had helped thousands of people with similar struggles turn those trials into strengths. I was actually overseeing the mental health, substance abuse, and sex offender treatment for all federal felons in the state where I lived. On a daily basis I helped people struggling with all sorts of challenges, and now I found myself facing a devastating trial I never saw coming and had been powerless to stop.

Then the most unbelievable thing happened to me. I was in the line greeting my brother's friends who came to pay their last respects, and I was unexpectedly blown over in the worst way. I suddenly found myself shaking the hand of the man that sexually abused me thirty-eight years earlier when I was eleven years old. Now he's telling me he was sorry? I was confused, in shock, and I couldn't move. A flood of memories and fear from my childhood made me freeze up. Another brother standing next to me noticed something was wrong because of my pale, blank stare and stepped between me and my perpetrator. Then I somehow managed to walk out of the church.

Despite all the knowledge, training, and resources available to me, I had been unable to help my brother find a way out of his internal despair. I couldn't help him see the family, friends, and options around him. My failure in helping my brother was so emotionally devastating and painful that it shook my foundation. A few weeks later I returned to work, trying to put on my usual face of strength, even though inside I was in turmoil. I continued to ask myself, "What more could I have done?" I promised to myself to do better at helping others. As the weeks turned into months, I continued to struggle with the loss of my brother and with other adversities that would follow during the year.

Then, as if by chance, something amazing happened. One night I was at home alone experiencing the typical stages of grief of shock, anger, and mild depression. I decided to act. I

PREFACE

began to review all the lessons I had taught others. I frantically pulled out all the handouts I had made over the past twenty years. I placed them next to each other on a ping pong table in my home. As I began reviewing my past life lessons, I began to feel hope. I started feeling better about my situation and could feel a change in myself. From that night, I began to heal, moving through towards acceptance and empowerment, the final stages of grief, instead of being caught in the cycle.

In that moment, it became crystal clear to me how my love of storytelling with visual lessons could be organized under one giant overarching visual picture of tapping a sugar maple tree. Over the years I had been willing to share my past failures and successes to individuals or small groups. Now I felt it was vital for me to overcome my fears once again and share my personal life's lessons with the world.

Over the years many people have given me the opportunity to help them move past trials and to grow stronger. Now I felt compelled to share what I had learned from people I have helped with an even broader audience. I realized if I could help just one person find the courage to grow stronger through their trials, it would be worth it. I decided to turn the year of heartache and devastation following my brother's death into something positive for my children, grandchildren, and anyone else who is willing to learn.

I realized that through this fresh experience with grief, I could now share my stories and insights with even more perspective, meaning, and empathy. Suddenly, I found I had a mission to write. I had a burning desire to help others avoid

PREFACE

giving up on life. I sensed that I could use my knowledge from overcoming this horrific and soul crushing experience to help others with their current trials. The answer was right before my eyes, and all I needed to do was to organize my stories and share them with others.

My plan was to organize my most useful stories in a simple way to help others. But I didn't stop there. I also started expressing my feelings, emotions, and struggles with my wife and eventually a therapist. I began spending every spare hour I could find, morning and night, writing my feelings and how I came up with each story.

Reviewing these lessons and recalling the change I had seen them make in my life and the lives of others gave me confidence. Although the lessons were somewhat unorganized, I realized I had tools that have worked for many, many people. I decided to formally organize those lessons to help even more people find hope. I found joy in the realization that if I could help people understand that they had already overcome trials in their lives, they could use or tap their past to help them with current or future trials.

My purpose in writing this book is to help you use my life's experiences and teachings to grow stronger from your own trials in life. In order to apply the teachings fully, you have some work to do. You'll not only want to read through the experiences and stories, but you'll want to really take in the visual lessons and answer the questions at the end of each chapter. This will help you internalize the information to the point that you can have it at your fingertips and, maybe, even teach it to someone

PREFACE

you care about. Then you can tap your trials and tell your story to others.

Those who have read this book and used the proven skills could call themselves "Trial Tappers." What is a Trial Tapper? It is anyone who wants to find hope in the future and is willing to recognize that all trials can produce growth. All you need to do is to tap a positive path.

This book will help you discover two things. First: Despite your trials, you have been able to grow strong enough to do many great things. Second: You have the strength within you to overcome any trial in life. Imagine how life could be different if you looked at each trial before you as an opportunity to grow stronger. What opportunities could trials provide you to help others? So many individuals I have worked with have found my visual stories helpful in moving past pain and towards growth. And that's why I'm so excited to share with you what it means to become a Trial Tapper, so you can get these types of results too!

Each of us has a different path in life, and each of us has our own trials or burdens to bear. I know how I feel when encountering a trial, but I DO NOT know how you feel. However, having said that, I can empathize with your trials. This book will introduce to you to my proven Trial Action Paths or TAPs.

Everyone has different learning styles. Some learn best by reading, some by visually using photos, and some by experiencing or doing something hands-on. As a visual learner, I have discovered that many people I work with are able to understand or relate to the visual stories I will share in this book. I have shared these with thousands of people, and now I share them with you.

The trial and pain of my brother's death has motivated me to share my experiences with you. By the end of the book, I hope you will know how you can overcome your unique struggles and become a Trial Tapper too. I know you can use the tools in this book to do just that. This book will help you grow resilient from trials and becoming stronger. This is not a book about death, but about LIFE! I have no desire to cause you more grief or secondary trauma. I will make every attempt to avoid graphic details and will infuse each story with hope instead. Your trials and experiences are unique as are mine, but together we may be able to find hope. Are you ready to move away from pain and towards a brighter future? Let's get started!

SECTION I
FOUNDATION

This section will help you understand the following:
What a Trial Tapper is.
Why I wrote this book.
Why I have included different stories and photos
to appeal to different learning styles.
How I developed the Trial Action Path (TAP) viewpoint
and how you can use it in your life.

• CHAPTER 1 •

Foundation

What Is a Trial Tapper?

First of all, let's get clear on the meaning of the words "Trial Tapper." In this book, when I use the word "trial," I am not referring to a courtroom with a judge. I'm referring to the struggles, challenges, setbacks, grief, loss, and conflict that we encounter throughout our lives. The word "tapper" as used in this book refers to the age-old profession of tapping trees for syrup. Similarly, we can tap into our own trials to increase in strength and wisdom. Trial Tappers take positive steps away from being a victim and towards being a survivor. They recognize that answers and growth can come from within themselves or with the help of others. They use positive actions and choose to take one of several proven paths to become stronger after any trial. A Trial Tapper will use one or more of the tools in this book to move away from pain and towards hope.

Another phrase you will see a lot of in this book is Trial Action Path or TAP for short. These are the tools that I have compiled to help you grow during and after any trial. Taking one of the TAPs will help you visualize finding strength inside you. There are many TAPs for you to choose from when preparing for and facing trials in this life.

How Does It Work?

This book will use the process of collecting maple tree sap as a metaphor or visual story to help you learn how to overcome your trials. A sugar maple tree needs to be tapped in order to collect sweet sap, which is hidden inside the tree. This sap is then processed into maple syrup. Much like a syrup tapper or farmer will actively drill into a maple tree to get to the sap, a Trial Tapper is someone that recognizes that answers and growth come from within. Over time, a Trial Tapper grows stronger and wants to share those positive paths with the world. By the end of this book I hope you can join me in becoming a Trial Tapper. Each visual story is helpful on its own, and all the lessons overlap or connect to each other. The primary visual story I will use to connect with the other stories is the concept of tapping a sugar maple tree for maple syrup.

Why did I choose sugar maple trees? Sugar maples are the major source of sap used for making maple syrup. Farmers will drill or tap a hole into a tree to access the sap, just as you will learn how to dig deep and access your potential inner growth. You can tap your inner potential. The way you can become a Trial Tapper is through your mindset by the way you look at trials in life.[1]

TRIAL TAPPERS

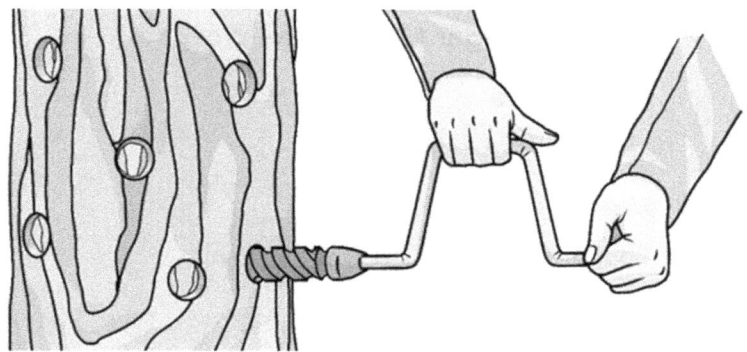

During harvest time, a farmer will use a hammer and hollow spike to tap into the inner-most part of the bark. This book will help you learn how to use tools and tap into your inner strength to become a Trial Tapper.

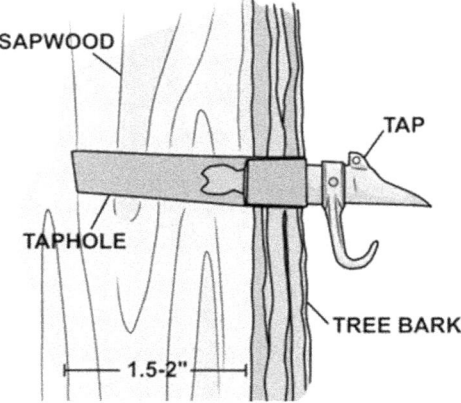

Tapping a sugar maple tree requires drilling a deep hole into the tree. Slowly the sap in the trees begins to drip out into collection buckets. Millions of drops of sap are collected and boiled down to produce the sweet maple syrup you use on your breakfast meals. As demonstrated in this illustration on how to collect sweet sap, I will show you how to turn trials into hope.

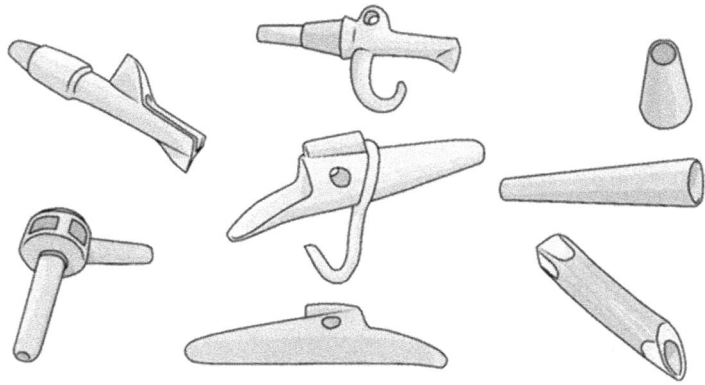

TRIAL TAPPERS

Farmers can use a variety of sugar maple tree taps to collect the sap. Similarly, I will show you a variety of tools I call Trial Action Paths (TAPs) to help you with life's challenges.

Just as maple trees have the hidden potential inside to produce sweet maple syrup, you have the ability to tap your past trials to produce positive growth. Using the visual story of tapping a maple tree, I will show you how to find the knowledge and resources in and around you to help you during a variety of trials in life.

Why I Wrote This Book

Let me begin by saying in this book I share my opinions and memories of how I experienced certain trials in my life. I don't have all the answers and often I will tell people, "I don't know why you had to go through this trial." You may have experienced common trials of life, or you may have experienced extremely horrific traumas no one should have to face. There may be no answers as to why. The hope is someday you will eventually find peace, although it may not be for many years to come. What I can tell you is that your successes in overcoming past trials have helped prepare you for the bigger challenges in your future, and you will need to rely on your past to help you through them.

Everyone I work with can identify some trial from their past that they have successfully overcome. As they look back on those challenges, often they will identify how those experiences are helping them now. This book will provide many informational tools to help you grow during and after a trial or trauma in your life. Upon completion of this book you should have the skills to find hope, a reduction in negative reactions to trials, and useful tools to help you adapt or find help to overcome your trials. This book is about understanding that you are strong enough to tap your trials to produce positive growth. I know you have dreams for success and can impact the world around you, and my purpose is to show you how to make that happen. This is why I wrote this book.

I have more than fifty years of life's experiences. As a child I dealt with physical growth challenges, bullying, shyness, sexual abuse, divorce, and impoverishment. As an adult I have dealt with vocal cord dysfunction, heart problems in my wife and son, the loss of a child due to miscarriage, the failure of a family business, and the loss of a brother due to suicide. However, I was fortunate enough to have the support of family, friends, and coworkers and the knowledge to get though the trials in life. This book will provide insight into how I have learned to deal with trials in life. I have built strong family relationships with my wife of twenty-six years and raised three wonderful boys. I became a federal probation officer, licensed clinical social worker and therapist, eventually overseeing the treatment of all federal felons in my state and in many other professional capacities. I'm a survivor, still learning and still growing!

As mentioned previously my younger brother committed suicide. The pain and anguish of this experience shook me to the core. I did all the typical and healthy things to survive. I cried a lot. I leaned on family, friends, co-workers. I did the symbolic rituals of writing a letter to my brother, attended his funeral, released hot air lanterns with those who loved him, and planted many flowers and maple trees in my yard in his honor.

I have been a therapist for more than twenty years and have helped thousands of people learn how to turn trials into strengths. I have worked with victims and perpetrators of sexual and physical abuse and have also specialized with people dealing with addictions. Although the trial I have mentioned, my brother's suicide was been very difficult, I will not focus on it in graphic detail. This is a book on how you can grow resilient from all trials in life.

Why You Should Read This Book

At times in life you might have asked yourself, "Why me? Why do these things have to happen to me or others I know? Why do we have to go through trials?" You might be wrestling with these questions right now. Trying to find the answers to these questions can be a lifelong journey.

Traumas and trials are part of the universal experience that we all must endure during this life. Often people come to see me because they are struggling with these questions as they face a trial, and they need help understanding "why." They ask themselves, their family, their friends, and even their God, "Why did this happen to me?"

If you've ever thought that there were people who delight because you are experiencing trials, you're probably right. Some people falsely believe that if you are succeeding, then they are failing. They want you to be miserable. However, know this: there are more people who actually care about your success and truly want to see you living the life of your dreams than there are people who want you to fail.

There's a little-known philosophy I created called the Trial Action Path (TAP) Viewpoint. When you learn how to use this tool, you'll see a huge difference in how you face trials. Knowing this one concept can change your life and those you care about.

WARNING! *Prepare for the Trial Action Path (TAP)*

The most important thing for you to remember is if you understand the Trial Action Path concept, it will help you for the rest of your life! The path or journey through pain is possible. This book is designed to give you strength if you are willing to recognize the past and look towards hope in the future! Growth from any trial will require some positive actions, and life will usually get harder before it gets better. The book may to be somewhat difficult to read from time to time, but it is designed to give you the tools to overcome any trials you might have or will experience in life.

Secondary Trauma is a term to describe how others who did not actually experience the event might be affected negatively when they hear about the event from others. As an empathetic person, you might feel sorry for me or others in this book. As you read both the trials and triumphs of others, you might possibly get emotional, recalling something similar to your life. Some stories are trials of poverty, finance, and health. Other stories deal with abuse or trauma from the death of loved ones.

Every effort will be made to avoid graphic or descriptive details of any event in this book. The stories are used to help you see the strength others have found after a trial or tragedy.

And just to be clear, this book is no substitute for therapy! It could be used in conjunction with therapy; however, you may not need to see a therapist. If so, then you should use this as a workbook to work through the trials and traumas in your life. Again, I reiterate that the growth process you will experience may get harder before it gets easier. You may experience a temporary decrease in happiness or an increase in discomfort. As you study, you might be going through a tough trial, and I commend you for starting this journey of hope. No one has been down your exact path; my trauma was not your trauma, but I believe you can find a path for hope and happiness once again.

Some of the best and hardest clients to help are those seeking help voluntarily. These clients don't have to be there and can stop when the pain gets too hard to face. Some choose therapy because they know there's a problem or someone close to them has pointed out their problems. Others are experiencing reactions and symptoms like anxiety, depression, anger outbursts, eating problems, addictions, etc. I hope you choose to voluntarily read this book, answer the questions, and seek help from others, if needed.

Reading this book might be a mental workout that is similar to a physical workout. When you first start working out and going to the gym, for example lifting weights, you may overdo it and stretch and strain your muscles. You will hurt for the next few days. In the following days, your mind may tell you to slow down or that this wasn't as fun as you thought it was going to be. But if you get up and go to the gym again day after day, it will get better. However, every time you lift a heavier weight, you will stretch those muscles again and feel physical pain for a little while until your body recovers. Anyone who's ever worked out will tell you it will get easier over time. The same is true with addressing instead of avoiding trials in your life. Eventually it will get easier to do. I'm sure you've noticed this too, right?

Another example is weight loss. When you diet to lose weight, the first five to ten pounds might come off quickly. But when you start working to lose the next fifteen to twenty pounds, it gets harder. You may want to give up and say ten pounds is good enough.

Much like physical workouts, when you emotionally exercise your internal thoughts, feelings, and emotions you are on the path of growth. You work on hard things by looking inward at yourself and examining the past.

Like weight loss and working out, the growth process of evaluating your life is tough. Don't give up!

Often, after I have worked with a client for about five sessions of therapy, suddenly they start canceling appointments and stop doing assignments; some will stop treatment altogether. They give a variety of excuses, such as, life got busy, something happened with my kids or with my work. Basically, some stop coming to treatment before they have truly made progress. I try to warn everyone that this may happen.

Many people would rather bury these painful feelings and emotions deep inside or conceal them with denial or mood-altering substances. If you're willing to take the challenge to grow from trials, remember it could get difficult for a while. Please take your time and understand that if you apply these skills and find supportive people, you will be stronger in the end because you have faced your trials.

The path to overcome any trial will require an action of deliberate, positive change. These actions will often be accompanied by additional struggles or challenges before positive growth and a return to happiness can occur. This growth path is demonstrated in the following chart called the Trial Action Path or the TAP viewpoint.

TAP Viewpoint

Most people going to therapy, or reading this book, are experiencing more of a decline in happiness than what they expected. This TAP warning predicts it might get tougher before it gets better; you will experience additional challenges. Each chapter addresses a different Trial Action Path or TAP.

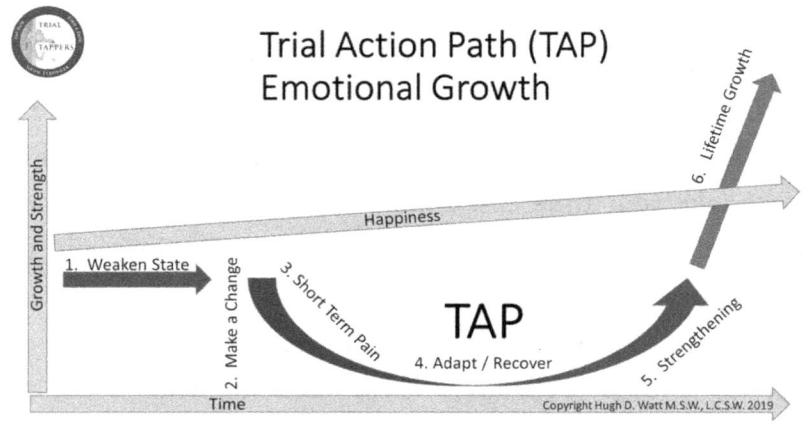

The illustration above (TAP Emotional Growth Chart) illustrates what you can expect to experience when you make the positive choice to address your traumas and trials. One: You may be in a weakened state of unhappiness. Two: Once you make the choice for positive change you will trigger an internal response of growth. Three: You may experience an increase in short-term emotional pain. You have heard the term, "No pain, No Gain"? TAP is the symbol indicating the potential discomfort. Four: You begin to grow, adapt to this new norm, and recover from the pain you are experiencing. You are now in the critical time of growth and will experience a new level of relief from the pain as your thoughts, feelings, and emotions become clear. Five: You will begin to understand the process of growth and recognize the strengths that will help you overcome this trial and future trials. Six: You will become satisfied with your progress towards a lifetime of growth from your trials. Happiness can increase after trials.

Identify the goal that you want to achieve. Find *Helpful Others* who can give you support along the journey. Expect that you may have setbacks and have to backtrack or even take another path. You should constantly monitor your happiness and be wary of those who try to bring you down. Finally, you need to be careful to focus your time and efforts on those things that you can control and avoid making "mountains out of mole hills" when possible. You can't control everything that happens to you, but you can control where you go from here.

The following are examples of events that can possibly intensify feelings of discomfort:

- Increased loneliness after the breakup of any relationship.
- Increased discomfort once you begin chemotherapy to fight cancer.
- Loss of income when you decide to leave a dead-end job and take one you like for less pay.
- Returning to college after twenty years to find you're required to repeat previous classes you already passed.
- You agree to testify against your assaulter in court and relive the past trauma.

The small trials are usually easy to talk about; but in order to achieve real growth, you must really dig deep and apply one or more of the following TAPs. Eventually, I hope you will get to the point in this book, (Stage 4 on the Emotional Growth Chart above), where you will be strong enough to start looking at trials as growth opportunities. You have overcome hard things in your past, and you can overcome this trial you are currently facing. Don't give up halfway through the process. Commit and be strong enough to say, "Okay, let's get to it. Let's get through it and prepare to survive future trials." One motto my family lives by is, "This too shall pass."

Understanding this section is vital to the rest of the book. In short, you will experience trials in life. When you choose to make a positive change, you will often experience a temporary decrease in happiness before a huge increase in your positive growth. You can expect this upfront cost, and the growth you will receive is absolutely worth it!

Why This Book Is Different

I have helped many people overcome trials in their lives. Some trials just happened to them, and some were self-created. This book is a culmination of life skills that I have learned and taught to thousands of people.

Why is this book different than other self-help books? I'm guessing that for a lot of you this is probably not the first self-help book you have read. The first thing I want you to understand is if you've failed at overcoming any trial in the past, it's not your fault. There are thousands of self-help books where people share their opinions on life. I have an entire library in my home of books that I've read. In many of them I have found one or two new ideas that have been helpful; others have multiple, helpful concepts. But if I'm honest with myself, I don't remember very much of what I have read. With so many different opinions, information overload keeps many from succeeding. It's okay.

I went to undergraduate school with a good friend, Christian Moore, and watched him develop the multi-sensory life skills program for struggling teens called *Why Try*. Years later, Christian allowed me to pilot this program with adults in the prison program Con-Quest. I eventually became a consultant, occasional presenter, and instructor for this program and found that multisensory learning was very effective. Upon completion of this book, I strongly recommend you read his book *The Resilience Breakthrough: 27 Tools for Turning Adversity into Action*. His book is a guide to resilience and, as he terms it, "the ability to bounce back from life's inevitable problems." Because many of my clients were visual learners, I eventually adapted the multisensory teaching style to all twenty-five courses in the Therapeutic Community (TC) Con-Quest, of which I was the director.

My success using visual lessons and TAP skills with others earned me prestigious awards and personal satisfaction. After being the director of the largest residential drug program in my state for more than six years, I was recruited to work with the federal court. This opportunity soon led to my being responsible for overseeing all treatment for federal felons coming out of prison in my state. Now I'm going to show you my secret formula and show you examples in each chapter of this book.

Review the image of the pyramid of learning below. It visually depicts that the lowest retention rate for learning/growth (in orange) is to have someone talk or lecture to you. The retention rate increases as you move down the pyramid, with the green level (90 percent) at the bottom representing the highest retention rate. You achieve a 90 percent retention rate of learning and growth by internalizing the lesson to the point that you can go and teach it to someone else. If you can teach it, you will remember it for life.

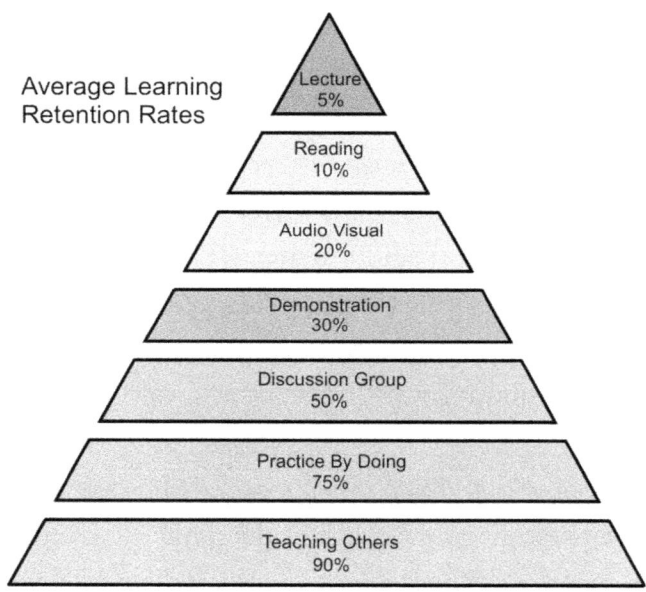

Memories of both good and bad experiences can be triggered by a smell or song. I love music and find it to be very powerful. In my office at work I listen to classical music all day, and it seems to calm me and anyone that comes into my office. When I worked in the prison system, I always asked the inmate bands to start each graduation off with the song "Lean on Me"

by Bill Withers. I strongly encourage you to stop reading this book and listen to the song now.

See what I mean? What memories do you associate with that song? Using more than one method of learning is much more impactful than reading alone. I have an entire playlist of uplifting music I listen to when I'm feeling down. I encourage you to do the same.

Some chapters are designed with simple exercises, and all have visual reminders to help you internalize these lessons for the rest of your life. I challenge you to complete the exercises included with each chapter. There are tangible life lessons to help you and those you care about to thrive in life despite the trials all will face.

Because repetition is an important part of learning, this book is designed with repetitive patterns to help you remember.

- I will introduce the lesson as a TAP.
- I will give examples of real-life stories in the form of a Trial Story.
- I will challenge you to reflect on what you have read/learned and decide where you are at on an Action Growth Scale from One to Ten; then ask you what it will take to move you up on the scale.
- I will ask you to answer the questions in the chapter.
- I will ask you to teach someone else what you have learned, as it relates to your life, to help someone else.

I know I am asking you to do a lot! I want you to understand the concepts and to remember them. If you fail to do things like answering questions and sharing what you have learned with others, you will forget more than 70 percent of what you read within a few weeks. You must participate in your learning and recovery to help yourself and others in the future. In order to help remind you of the skills you learn in this book, I have also created a one-of-a-kind deck of daily growth cards. These daily growth cards will help you recall what you have learned. An example of these cards is included at the end of this book. I encourage you to also obtain these simple memory tools.

If you want to learn how to master a new skill, such as playing a musical instrument, you will have to practice. Just listening to someone play music and showing you how to play will not help much. Sure, it will sound good and you can tell everyone you "understand" how the instrument works, but you will not be capable of playing anything recognizable until after you practice a lot. The approach set forth in this book is to practice by answering all the questions at the end of each chapter and then teaching what you have learned to others. Doing this will help you remember up to 90 percent of what you are learning in this book.

Like all plants, a maple tree has to struggle to grow stronger every year until it is large enough to begin producing sap for maple collection. This tree will endure many harsh winters and freezing weather. The growth of any tree will be measured in gradual inches over time.

Each tree has three choices as it faces the seasons: First, to barely survive in a weakened state; second, to reach a certain height and stop growing; or third, to adapt to the storms of the seasons and grow more vibrant and strong every year, reaching its potential and producing usable sap for collection to benefit others.

Be active in your *Resilient Growth Actions* is illustrated by a 10-inch ruler measuring the growth of a maple tree branch. The ruler is divided into three sections. Inches 1–3 are labeled Weaken State. Inches 4–7 are labeled No Growth Neutral. The final inches, 8–10, are labeled Strong Growth.

This same illustration will be repeated at the end of every chapter in this book. When you see this image, identify where you are on the growth scale as it relates to each lesson. Try to identify how you will move up the scale into the Strong Growth section.

How This Book Can Help You

Tired of struggling from one trial to the next? Do you feel like no one knows how to help you with trials? Do you hate how long it takes to feel happy after facing a difficult trial? The TAP viewpoint changes the way you face any trial. Understanding the paths in this book will amaze everyone around you as you not only survive but thrive after any trial. The goals of this book are: First, to help you recognize you have overcome many trials in the past; second, recognize that you can overcome future trials; and third, give you the insight and tools to allow you to teach others how to overcome their trials.

The reality of life is that trials happen to all of us. But what few people understand is the idea that, with the passing of time, you can use those trials to produce growth. This might be hard to believe but you can become stronger in spite of any trial you are experiencing now or will experience in the future.

Understanding how simple it is to use these TAPs, these very specific tools, in your life will change the way you view the future. Those who aren't aware of these tools are at risk of struggling with trials longer than necessary. Even worse, they may fail to grow from the experience. I have spent my entire life helping people overcome trials. I have both professional and personal experience applying my proven steps. Learning the TAP viewpoint and how to apply the TAPs included within this program is the key to gaining happiness more quickly after any trial. I have designed this book to be more than just a book of nice visual stories. I share experiences from my life and the lives of family, friends, coworkers, and others whom I've seen overcome their trials. Then I ask you to answer a few questions for yourself as you read. You can answer them in your mind, but it will be more effective if you write down your answers. These are not all the questions I normally use with helping people. If you want more than what I have provided here, you should seek out my certification class with supporting manual and handouts.

Are you ready to get started?

Share What You Learn with Others

It is vital for you to share what you have learned with others. If you can teach each concept to others in a way they can understand, using your own examples, you will remember the lesson the rest of your life. You can also journal about what you're learning, and I hope that by the time you are done reading, you will be ready to share with others. My favorite movie is *The Power of One* released in 1992. It is an inspiring story about a boy who grows up in South Africa during apartheid and eventually begins to teach people to read. This movie demonstrates how one person can make a huge difference to others when they dare to share what they have learned.

What Are TAP Stories?

A TAP Story is a story that illustrates a Trial Action Path (TAP) that someone I know has faced in life. This story will identify which *Resilient Growth Actions* were used to overcome the trial. It will be introduced by the following visual.

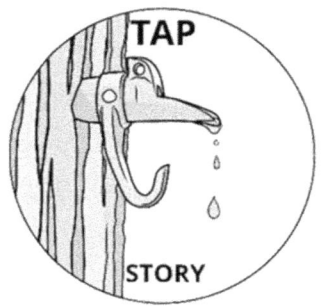

Each chapter in this book will share the initial trial, then the additional trials that came, and then the actual growth the individual achieved or may possibly achieve with future growth or inner strength with the help of others. Again, you will understand these terms more once you complete the book.

How to Take What You Have Learned from Reading This Book to the Highest Level of Retention

Listen to your thoughts as you read and answer the questions. Pay attention to your thoughts and feelings, even those unrelated to the visual lesson you are reading.

Ask questions as you read. As you read, questions may come to your mind. Ponder these questions and look for answers as you continue studying.

Share what you have learned. Discussing insights from your learning not only helps others, but also helps you grow in your understanding of what you have read. Summarizing what you have learned in your own words will help you remember the lessons.

Commit to positive actions. I hope you know you have overcome trials in your life and are prepared to demonstrate growth by your actions. Commit to positive actions in the future and apply these new skills in your life.

Create your own story. Once you are finished with this book, you will notice new visual lessons all around you to help teach lessons to yourself and others. Your learning should grow well beyond reading this book.

Be open-minded, flexible, and actively learn. Some questions asked in this book you will not be able to answer at first. If you come across a question that does not relate, just move on and consider returning to the question when you have had time to think about it for a few hours or days.

Ponder the TAP stories of others. Each chapter will provide you with at least one trial story about someone who faced a struggle and used the TAP concepts for growth. If you can't relate to the story, consider other people you know and how they used a similar lesson in their lives. Ultimately, I hope you can fill in your own TAP story that relates to the lesson. You have grown from past trials, and you can use those lessons learned to overcome future trials.

Measure your growth. This book has a main story of a growing sugar maple tree as the background to teach you skills to grow after any trial. After each chapter you will be asked to identify where you are on the growth chart as it relates to that visual lesson. You will have a scale from 1 to 10. Be honest in your initial self-rating. Then work to increase to a higher level on the growth scale.

Record thoughts and feelings and make commitments to yourself. Take the time to write down your thoughts by answering the questions in the chapter. You may decide to keep a separate journal of your thoughts as you study this book.

I will provide you with memorable stories, pictures, and questions for you to answer. The final question in each chapter will ask you to record your thoughts, things you're grateful for, and commitments to positive actions. I'm going to make it easy for you. I will show you several TAPs that specifically apply to your life. You then get to decide which ones will work for you. Are you understanding how this works?

What I Hope You Learn from Reading This Book

As I look back on my life and career and write this book, I marvel at where I've come from and what I've accomplished. I have tapped into the traumas and trials of my life and turned those struggles and pains into something positive. My unique upbringing and responses to those trials has put me on a course away from dysfunction and towards healing for myself and others.

In the following chapters I will describe how you can become resilient after any trial. I hope you realize you have overcome challenges in your past and can use those lessons to help you overcome trials in the future. By the time you finish this book, I hope you will appreciate these visual stories and understand how to apply several TAPs in your life. When you have completed this book you should be able to teach anyone how each visual lesson can relate to their life.

One question might be, "What is your purpose in reading this book?" If your purpose is to learn skills in order to help others with their trials, you will have many tools available when you're finished. However, if your purpose is to overcome a very specific trial you are experiencing, these tools might help you do that, as will a professional therapist, depending on the intensity of the trial or trauma.

What you get from this book will depend on what life-lens you are looking through as you read and answer the questions. If your current trial is with addiction (drugs, sex, eating, money, etc.), anxiety, or depression, you might conclude that this book helped you deal with addiction, anxiety, and depression. If your trial is a self-harming behavior, you might conclude that it helped you overcome those issues, struggles, difficulties, or behaviors. Ultimately, this book was written with the purpose of allowing you the flexibility to use these skills to overcome any trial.

Please read with an open mind. If some stories or examples don't exactly relate to your current situation, they may relate to what someone you care about is experiencing. I challenge you to apply these lessons in your life and to teach others how to turn their trials into something positive. Upon completing this book, you still might not know why you faced these trials, but I hope you will have developed the skills to tap inner strength and grow stronger.

The process of using the TAPs is designed for anyone to follow. If you don't think your can do it on your own, I hope you will eventually seek help from others like family, friends, clergy, and/or therapists. Your first action for growth will be to read and honestly answer the questions in this book. It might be hard for you to believe you can find answers to your life's trials, but I will walk you through it in each of the following chapters. You will soon see that these chapters have similar patterns that make the TAPs easy to remember and apply in your life. Imagine what your life could be like as you grow stronger after your trials!

SECTION II
SAFETY & GROUND SUPPORTS

These chapters will provide lessons about the following concepts:
You are not alone in your trials
and how to identify those willing to help you.
Trials make you stronger and growth is possible from any trial.
You can prepare for trials and look forward to the future.

• CHAPTER 2 •

TAP #1: Tap Your Life's Trials – We ALL Have Pain!

*"Your trials in this life are unique,
but trials are not unique in life."*

TAP Overview: This TAP presents the concept that your trials in life are unique. The visual example of tapping sugar maple trees illustrated herein will be the connecting link to all the stories or TAPs in this book. Research proves you are not alone. This TAP will also teach you that (1) Growth after any trial should be measured and (2) Growth is both physical and emotional.

Please, make sure you have reviewed the introductory pages. Although you may think the introduction is not important, it contains vital instructions on how to use this book. If you skip it, you will miss essential information. It will be almost like baking a cake without following the step-by-step instructions. The specific outline and organization of this book is designed to provide you with maximum retention and growth. So please take a few minutes to go back and read the introduction. Thank you. If you did not skip the introduction, I say, "Good job!"

To begin, the image on the cover of this book and shown above shows a maple tree growing in the forest with two maple collection buckets hanging from maple taps. Hidden from view are hundreds of trees, each with their own buckets hanging from maple taps. This maple tree, and the process of collecting sap to make maple syrup, will be used as the visual example to help you overcome trials throughout this book.

The process of making pure maple syrup is very labor-intensive. Thousands of years ago indigenous people discovered that as spring approached, the sap in maple trees began to travel from the roots to the tops of the trees. They discovered if they scraped or cut the tree, pure maple water would drip out. Over time creative farmers found that if they drilled a small hole about one inch in diameter into the trunk of the tree, they could hammer a small metal spigot or tap into the hole, and then hang a metal bucket on the tap to collect the sap.

Collecting maple sap from trees is called sugaring and takes time and patience. The general rule of thumb is that it takes forty parts of boiled-down maple sap to produce one part of maple syrup. Or in other words, forty gallons of sap to produce one gallon of syrup, or ten gallons of sap to produce one quart of syrup. However, these estimates are dependent on the amount of sugar content in the sap. The sap that is collected is like water with a slight hint of maple sweetness. Pure organic maple water is in many grocery stores. I encourage you to get a sample to try for yourself. The bottle pictured here is a close representative of an actual bottle.

There's an old saying, "You can't see the forest through the trees." Again, what you do not see on the cover page is the hundreds, if not thousands, of trees that farmers must tap in order to collect enough sap for production. The tree in this chapter is surrounded by other unseen trees each with their own taps or trials.

The visual image of using taps to slowly collect drops of sap into a bucket, I believe, is symbolic of how we experience trials in this life. A maple tree in the forest grows spontaneously, and it is unknown when or where someone will drill into it and hammer in the maple tap. It will endure many storms throughout its life as it grows to a point where it can produce maple sap for collection. Tapping a tree does not kill it, and most recover well.

The experience or trial of this tree is similar to the trials and storms we will endure in life. We don't choose where we grow up or the circumstances around us as we grow. We have no idea when someone will tap us with a trial. At first, the pain of the tap may cause us to shed tears similar to the drops of sap falling into the bucket. Just as that sap will have to endure a boiling fire to produce sweet things for others to enjoy, we can endure the trials and taps in our life and grow to the point where our trials will make us stronger and provide us the opportunity and ability to help others experiencing trials in their lives.

Your trials in life will be unique to you. The trauma, pain, and sorrow from your trial will be undeniable and personal. But just as this tree which is being tapped in the forest is not alone, know that you are not alone in this world as you experience trials. Everyone will go through pain and their own individual life struggles in areas such as financial, health, employment, relationships, abuse, addictions, etc.

Although it is no secret that we all have trials, many people suffer alone in silence. The challenge in life is to know how to use positive tools to turn the pains of those trials into something useful for the future.

If you were to step back and look at the unseen trees in the forest, you would see that some trees have more taps and buckets on them than others. And although it sometimes appears that you are going through more trials than those around you, this may not be the case.

I often tell my clients that are struggling to overcome a trauma or trial, "I don't know why you are experiencing this pain. I don't know how you are feeling, and I don't know what we are going to learn from this trial. But I do know that we can get through it together using proven tools for success."

Likewise, I will use my expertise to teach you the tools you need to overcome this current trial and any trial in the future. I will use many other visual stories in this book to teach these tools, but the general visual of maple trees and maple taps will be used to help you grow stronger after any trial. I use this analogy, in combination with proven theory and concepts, to help you visualize the process we will go through.

If you were to plant a maple tree, you would want to rely on the expertise of the weather service to help you prepare for and predict future storms. Despite your efforts to prepare, ultimately storms come to everyone in one form or another.

Why do we fear trials? Why do we compare our trials and our responses to them to others? Why are we afraid to tell others we are experiencing trials? Why are we afraid to ask for help from others?

Answer? You don't understand your power, strength, and ability as a Trial Tapper.

Millions of others around you are experiencing trials and traumas. You might not care to see the research, but understanding that there are many people around you that have and will experience traumas is important. Just know many people struggle with trauma in life and go on to do many amazing things.

The *Centers for Disease Control and Prevention (CDC)-Kaiser Permanente Adverse Childhood Experiences (ACE) Study* was one of the largest studies of childhood abuse and neglect and, later, life health and well-being. This study, conducted from 1995 to 1997, collected over 17,000 confidential surveys during physical exams regarding childhood experiences.[1]

What did they find out?

Adverse Childhood Experiences (ACE) are common. Almost two-thirds of study participants reported at least one adverse childhood event, and more than one in five reported three or more of these events. As the number of childhood events increases, so does the risk for the following. Note that this list is not exhaustive.

- Alcoholism and alcohol abuse
- Chronic obstructive pulmonary disease
- Depression
- Fetal death

---

[1] Source: Centers for Disease Control and Prevention, Kaiser Permanente. The ACE Study Survey Data [Unpublished Data]. Atlanta, Georgia: U.S. Department of Health and Human Services, Centers for Disease Control and Prevention; 2016.

- Health-related quality of life
- Illicit drug use
- Ischemic heart disease
- Liver disease
- Poor work performance
- Financial stress
- Risk for intimate partner violence
- Multiple sexual partners
- Sexually transmitted diseases
- Smoking
- Suicide attempts
- Unintended pregnancies
- Early initiation of smoking
- Early initiation of sexual activity
- Adolescent pregnancy
- Risk for sexual violence
- Poor academic achievement

SAMHSA-HRSA Center for Integrated Health Solutions explains it in this way.[2]

> Trauma. Individual trauma results from an event, series of events, or set of circumstances experienced by an individual as physically or emotionally harmful or life-threatening with lasting adverse effects on the individual's func-

---

[2] Source: www.integration.samhsa.gov/clinical-practice/trauma

tioning and mental, physical, social, emotional, or spiritual well-being.

In the United States, 61 percent of men and 51 percent of women report exposure to at least one lifetime traumatic event, and 90 percent of clients in public behavioral health care settings have experienced trauma. If trauma goes unaddressed, people with mental illnesses and addictions will have poor physical health outcomes and ignoring trauma can hinder recovery.

So, what does this all mean? You and I are not alone in experiencing trials! Almost two-thirds of the study participants reported at least one adverse childhood experience of physical or sexual abuse, neglect, or family dysfunction. And more than one of five reported three or more such experiences. Trauma is a near-universal experience in life, and failure to address or resolve your past may have already had or can have major consequences on your health in the future.

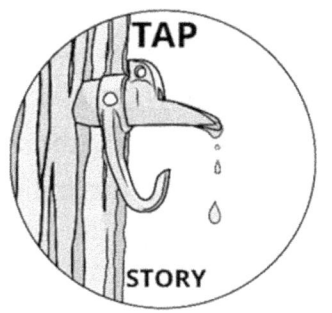

TAP Story: My Mother's Childhood

TRIAL TAPPERS

Main TAP Tool: Life's Trials

Low Point/Stress Point: How can I survive a divorce?

Trial Story: As confirmed by the research above, my mother was raised in a very chaotic family similar to more than 25 percent of the women reported in the study. The abuse in the home was real and caused her much heartache and self-doubt. Without support or direction in the home, this culture of few rules left her looking for direction. At the age of fifteen a kind family welcomed her into their home under a voluntary foster care program. Finally, she had a family that had religious morals and rules that my mother was looking for in life. This family raised my mother in a kind and loving way that provided support and direction until she turned eighteen and got married.

Soon after she was married my father was called up to serve in the Vietnam War. I was born, and my mother was forced to care for me until he completed his service. Separation is never good for a young new couple, and my parents struggled for many years to make the marriage work. Despite their efforts, their marriage only lasted about thirteen years before they separated and finally divorced. The divorce was devastating on my mother, and she was left to raise the children on her own. My mother eventually remarried, and she decided to adopt two infant boys from mothers that had their own "colorful" lives but chose to give their children a better life.

As is very common, this second marriage came with its own challenges, and my mother finally divorced this man several years later. Being divorced twice was very challenging on her ego, but she eventually recovered from the pain. After many years alone she finally met her third husband and is very happy in this relationship. Sadly, my mother later lost her adopted son Cody to the devastation and pain of suicide. This loss far outweighed the pain of her two divorces, and yet with time she is becoming stronger. She has survived many traumas, but nevertheless the past trials in her life have made her stronger each time.

Growth Actions: The point here is that foster care helped my mother find safety and support. Divorce was challenging for her, but it led to her adopting two more beautiful children. My mother is now able to help those that lose others to death. I hope this book will help her in the growth process of overcoming this latest trial. My mother is strong and has survived many trials in her life.

TAP to Strong Growth: My mother survived the funeral but now needs to survive the holidays, missed birthdays, and anniversaries of her son's death.

TAP to a Lifetime of Growth: I don't know why my mother had such a hard life, but I do know she eventually became the adoption specialist for the State of Utah. Some of the greatest joys she had were setting up appointments and meetings to help reconnect adopted children with their birth parents after they reached the age of eighteen.

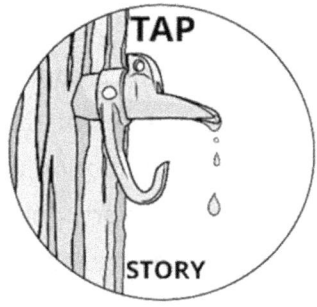

TAP Story: My Growth
Main TAP Tool: Resilient Growth
Low Point/Stress Point: Why are you so short?
Trial Story: As a young boy my lack of physical growth was a constant worry. The thing was, as a child I struggled to physically grow, and I was always at the lowest end of the height scale. At age of five I endured what some would consider barbaric medical testing only to discover that my body was not producing much growth hormone. The tests involved injecting me with insulin to almost produce a physical state of confusion that bordered on the edge of seizures in the hope that my pituitary glands would produce enough growth hormone to be measured. Afterward, a medical team did blood tests to see if this procedure worked. After enduring these tests multiple times in the day as a small child, I became traumatized towards hospitals and especially needles.

Test results identified the problem that my body was producing very little growth hormone. Although my family attempted to compensate for the fact that I was the shortest person in all my classes growing up, they could not protect me from bullying. As often will occur to the shortest person in a school, bigger kids found it comical to tease, taunt, and bully me. I can still remember the names of those elementary boys that teased me, yet I will not dishonor them by mentioning their names here. Bullying was very devastating to my self-esteem, and I became very shy as a result of the teasing. When I was a boy, the Saturday morning cartoons had a character called "Baby Huey." The ironic thing was the show's character was a very large and oversized person. The timing of this could not have been worse for me. I can still hear the teasing on the playground: "Hey, Baby Huey."

Growth Actions: At age twelve my doctor told my mother and me that it appeared that I had stopped growing a few years before. During a routine doctor visit around the time my parents' divorce, my pediatrician took interest in my plight and wanted to help me grow taller than four feet eleven inches. He told my mom and me that researchers had found some new experimental drugs to help me grow. Something miraculous began to happen. Over the next year, this medicine helped me grow six inches to my final height of five feet five inches tall. Growing this fast does not come without extreme growing pains. Although I am still short, it's better than my originally projected four feet eleven inches.

TAP to Strong Growth: Through this experience, I learned a lot about medical procedures as a child. I learned that bullying did not define me. I learned to focus on things I could control.

TAP to a Lifetime of Growth: The point I am making is that no matter where I go, I am often still the shortest man in the group. I learned early on that I had to use more brain than brawn to deal with bullies. Fortunately, the fact that I was shorter than most people became less and less of an issue as I went to college. Like most trials, sometimes we don't understand how we have emotionally grown from those experiences until much later in life. Once I married and had children, I realized I could use my past experiences to help my second child.

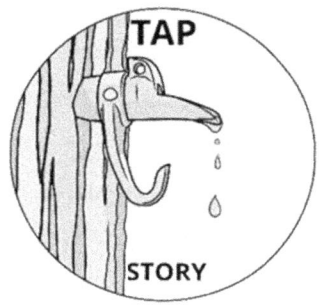

TAP Story: My Son's Growth
Main TAP Tool: Resilient Growth Actions
Low Point/Stress Point: The doctor just told us that our son was unusually short.
Trial Story: One of my worst fears came true when the doctor told my wife and me that my second son inherited the same growth hormone deficiency that I have. Fortunately, we recognized this early and worked with doctors to begin the required treatment in the form of growth hormone shots. This news came with the worry of the treatment ahead, but the hope that bullying would someday end.
Growth Action: Once the problem was identified, deciding to proceed with the medical tests was temporarily worse than

ignoring the problem. The huge hurdle was, in order to qualify for the treatment, my son had to endure similar terrible procedures of fasting, blood draws, and injections in order to prove to our insurance company that the $15,000 dollars-a-month medication was necessary and would work. I felt sad hearing my son talk about being teased in school due to his size, and now I was reliving my past traumas of doctors. At a young age my son had to learn that he was going to need daily shots so that he could grow, and I was going to have to overcome my fear of needles to help him. My son knew he was short - kids are cruel and teased him about his height - but my childhood experience gave us hope that this could work for him. For the next several years, my son endured the daily shots and their side effects that included passing out, blood sugar levels dropping, and requiring special attention from each teacher. He faced all this as a young boy with the hope it would all pay off with additional growth some years in the future. The pain he had to experience each day was hard for my young son to understand as the results were very slow to see. Eventually by age sixteen, with the help of those daily shots, my son was able to reach the same height as myself, about five feet five inches.

TAP to Strong Growth: My son was born with very little growth hormone and yet he overcame this challenge. He learned to endure daily shots. He overcame bullying in his childhood. He Survived!

TAP to a Lifetime of Growth: We worry this condition will be passed on to his children. If this is the case, I know my son has grown both physically and emotionally from this experience. In the past we measured his growth in physical inches, but we now recognize how he has grown emotionally because of this experience. My son turned this TAP into a positive. As an adult he has developed a strong sense of empathy towards others that struggle with a variety of personal challenges. I am especially proud of how he interacts with others he knows who struggle with mental and physical challenges. He now works as a pharmacy technician and is studying to become a pharmacist. Will he be able to help other doctors learn about the medications needed for children lacking growth hormones? Will he find a cure for other kids facing this problem? His potential growth is unlimited.

In the TAP stories above I shared how my mother navigated a troublesome family life to eventually help others build strong families through adoption. I also shared the trial both my son and I had with physical growth, an experience that forced us to become resilient from bullying and emotionally grow strong. This first TAP will ask you to identify your growth in a specific trial and then use this same measurement for the remaining taps in this book.

Now this is the part of the book where I ask you to do something for yourself besides read. I ask you to answer questions about your life. I also encourage you to write your impressions in the spaces provided in this book. Your answers to the questions in this book can be stated in just a few words.

Imagine you are this maple tree that has endured two maple taps to gather sap for syrup. You do not stand in the forest to face these trials and storms in life alone. Everyone experiences individualized trials, but you can turn these pains into strengths by learning how others have grown from trauma and trials.

1. This tree has a trial. What is the most obvious trial you are facing now?

2. This is not the first storm for the tree. List three other trials you have overcome in life.

3. Imagine a miracle happens and your trials are removed. How will your life be better?

4. Envision a small trial you successfully overcame. What four steps did you take to achieve success?

5. What organization can you seek guidance from to overcome this trial?

Wasn't that easy? You can do the same for all chapters. Doing so will greatly improve your learning, recall, and growth.

Internalization: Help Someone – Go and Teach Someone this Life TAP.

Note: Growth after a trial is measured in small steps. The growth of a tree branch is measured in inches. Identify where you are now on this scale as it relates to a trial you are experiencing. Then mark where you want to be and take steps towards post-trial growth.

1. List a positive goal in an area you can control.

2. What short-term steps can you take to move closer to your goal?

3. Mark on this scale where you are now with the belief you can achieve this goal (Weakened State, No Growth – Neutral, or Strong Growth).

4. What will motivate you to move up one level?

5. What progress towards your goal can you make today?

This Growth Chart will be a helpful tool after every chapter to determine where you are with the skill being taught.

Record your thoughts...

_____
_____
_____

Record what you are grateful for...

_____
_____
_____

Record your commitment to positive action...

_____
_____
_____

Recap: Growth after any trial should be measured. Your learning can be increased using multisensory learning styles. Teaching others is the highest form of learning. Growth is both physical and emotional.

As a Trial Tapper I see trials as TAPS and chances to grow.

• CHAPTER 3 •

TAP #2: Tap Your Season of Symptoms – S.O.S.

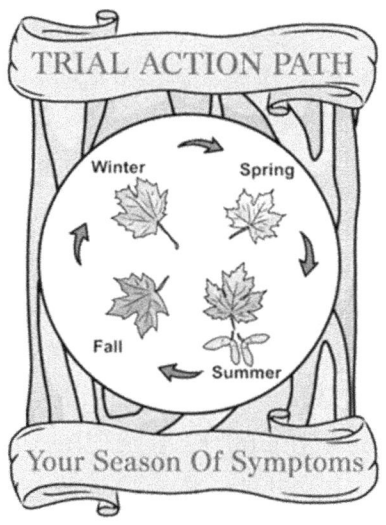

*"The effects of the seasons are easily seen,
yet understanding the roots of your symptoms are often screened."*

TAP Overview: This TAP will demonstrate that different times of the year are more challenging for some than others. Anniversaries, birthdays, or holidays can be difficult reminders of particular trials. This TAP will help you work to treat the real problem, not just the symptoms. Sometimes all you need to do is take a few deep breaths. This TAP will also explain that if you review the events in your life you will see that you have had both good and bad experiences. Many trials can be reframed from negative to positive experiences with the passing of time. This chapter will help you identify, not only the trials you may have faced, but also the positive things you have and will experience in life.

Tap Your Season of Symptoms – S.O.S. is the next visual illustration. This image shows four maple leaves at different stages of growth. The top right leaf is light green and labeled "Spring." The downward pointing arrow on the right leading to a dark green leaf with two seed pods attached is labeled "Summer." The arrow at the bottom of the image points to a red leaf labeled "Fall." The arrow on the left points up to a brown leaf labeled "Winter." Finally, the arrow at the top of the image completes the repetitive circle of the seasons.

The health of any tree requires that nutrients in the earth to be processed by the roots of the tree. The sap travels up from the roots to the trunk of the tree and eventually to the branches to produce growth in the leaves.

Consider the seasons during the year and how they affect a tree. During the spring, the fresh green leaves bud out of the branches. As spring turns to summer, the leaves turn dark green and begin to develop seed pods. As summer turns to fall, the leaves begin to turn red, orange, and yellow. Then as fall turns to winter, the leaves lose their bright colors, fade to brown, and eventually fall to the ground.

The signs and stages of the leaf of the maple tree are predictable and progress with the passing of time. Weather is the main cause of the changes. When the weather warms, it signals to the tree roots to begin producing sap. When the weather cools, it signals to the tree to stop producing sap, and the leaves begin to die.

This TAP, *Season of Symptoms*, is also labeled S.O.S., a word play on the radio call sign for help or distress. S.O.S. represents the reason you might be reading this book or why you might be considering going to a therapist. You might need help, or you might know someone that is crying for help.

When my clients show up needing help for a reason that is unknown to me, I will often ask questions like: "Why are you here today? What problem brought you here today? How can I help you?" Then I listen to the initial identified problem.

Few clients begin explaining the root or real problem. Instead they disclose general symptoms such as stress, anxiety, depression, addictions, or other harmful behaviors. These are often observable symptoms that they notice about themselves or that others have identified as a problem, such as being unable to keep a job or stay in a relationship. Sometimes family or the legal system will point out harmful behaviors such as addictions or arrests.

It is important to determine the root problem, not just treat the symptom. For example, a conviction for Driving under the Influence (DUI) is not specifically a drinking problem. A good therapist will explore the thoughts, feelings, and emotions that led up to the excessive drinking and decision to drive a car. Having typical reactions to trials and trauma is not a sign of weakness, but when these reactions become harmful to yourself or others, you know you need help. When your reactions impair your ability to perform normal daily activities and responsibilities or endanger yourself or others, you need to seek professional help.

If you realize you need help from a professional, only focusing on your symptoms and how to stop them will waste your time and money. For example, a young therapist might attempt to teach you anger management skills without understanding that the root of the anger stems from being abused as a child. Another might advocate meditation as a way to deal with your anxiety yet fail to recognize that your anxiety is caused by living in a controlling and abusive relationship.

You could spend weeks, months, or years in therapy discussing symptoms without discovering the root problem. With the passing of time those symptoms may lessen, and you and perhaps your therapist may conclude that therapy is no longer needed. If you were really concentrating on the root problems, a few weeks or months of therapy might be sufficient. However, only focusing on symptoms is probably a waste of time. Just understand that the therapist can only work with what you tell them.

Don't be fooled into thinking that you have resolved some past trauma. As the seasons cycle throughout the year, a tree will eventually end up dormant, not showing any signs of life. Your signs and symptoms can eventually go back into hibernation until you experience a similar trauma or enter the same season during the year. Why would your symptoms appear to be gone for a season and then reappear? If you don't truly address the root cause, they could come back because you have avoided the real problem and chosen not to address it. You might have buried the problem deep inside and avoided or replaced the problem with other behaviors or habits or, even worse, covered it up by abusing substances. The following exercises will help you identify whether you repeatedly experience telling symptoms during the same time of the year. If you have this predictable pattern or the symptoms grow increasingly worse over time, you may not be addressing the root problems.

One example of only focusing on the symptoms rather than the root problem would be participating in medically assisted detox from drugs without participating in behavioral therapy. Some believe if they remove the drug from their blood, they won't crave or return to the same behaviors they relied on in the past to cope with their life's trials. The sad reality is, just as the seasons predictably change, returning to old patterns of coping with life's challenges may lead to a return to use of and possibly overdose on drugs. The symptom of addiction requires exploring the root behaviors leading to the addiction.

I'm responsible for approving therapy for hundreds of people each year. When clients tell me they are struggling with certain symptoms, I often refer them simultaneously to both a doctor and a therapist to address the symptoms. The doctor may prescribe medications to address some of the symptoms, but the therapist will be able to spend hours with you exploring the root problem.

It is not uncommon for unwanted symptoms or physical reactions to intensify during the actual season of the year when a big trial or trauma occurred. Which season causes you the most trouble will depend on your life's experiences. The loss of a family member could make the winter holidays difficult. A past traumatic abuse that occurred in the summer may cause recurring nightmares each July. Many people who suffer with depression have difficulty in the winter. However, although the holidays can be difficult for many who have experienced a trial or trauma, I'm always concerned about their actions during the fall and spring. According to the Centers for Disease Control and Prevention (CDC), suicide rates spike in the spring and fall, not around the holidays as many suspect. The suicide rate is, in fact, the lowest in December.[3]

Experiencing some seasonal symptoms is typical on anniversaries of your past trials, as you may never forget some of the worst events. If the symptoms cause increasing discomfort, perhaps you have a root problem that needs to be investigated with the assistance of a professional therapist. The first step is to realize that you need assistance dealing with the unwanted symptoms. Family or friends may point out your repeated behaviors, moods, or signs and symptoms that seem to be out of character for you. Pay attention to what others are saying and

---

[3] Centers for Disease Control and Prevention. Web-based Injury Statistics Query and Reporting System (WISQARS) [Online]. (2008) National Center for Injury Prevention and Control, Centers for Disease Control and Prevention (producer). Available from:
URL: http://www.cdc.gov/violenceprevention/suicide/holiday.html.

avoid being offended or dismissive to their observations or concerns.

As a therapist, I would often find missed signs and symptoms when I worked with victims of sexual abuse. I was amazed at the parent's reactions when they were told of the abuse. Some were in denial and admitted that they knew something was wrong but would not believe the obvious signs. Others were victims themselves as children and regressed into a state of justification, acceptance, or denial. I don't want you to miss possible signs of abuse in children around you.

Many behavioral signs and symptoms of abuse in children can be found on Internet sites. These may include nightmares, bedwetting, depression, anxiety, poor hygiene, failing, running away, suicide attempts, etc. Although not all these behaviors are the result of sex abuse, you might consider a professional therapist for a child demonstrating some of these signs.

When I went to therapy, I identified a major problem that was deeply painful: my brother's suicide. I needed to talk to someone about this problem because of the internal symptoms I was experiencing in my life: sorrow, grief, irritability, being overwhelmed, and sleeplessness that are often the body signaling that it needs professional help. My family and friends saw my obvious symptoms of frustration and anger. I knew I wanted to address the underlying issue of grief, pain, and regret that was causing physical manifestations of anger, sleeplessness, and irritability.

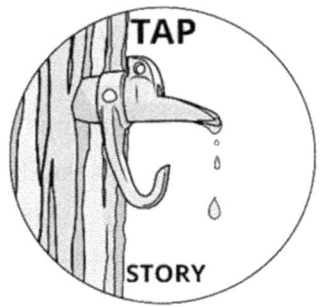

TAP Story: Granddaughter's Lung Problem
Main TAP Tool: Season of Symptoms
Low Point/Stress Point: The ultrasound revealed your baby has a problem.

Trial Story: My oldest son and his wife were excited to announce that they were expecting their second child, my granddaughter. Soon the signs of the pregnancy were easy to see. My daughter-in-law was experiencing all the typical signs of being pregnant including nausea and a baby bump. Within a few months, the excitement of a having new baby changed as the family came to a terrible realization of how fragile life can be. An ultrasound revealed that my future granddaughter had a mass growing on her lung. Doctors informed us that if she didn't start growing faster than the mass in her lung, she would not survive. I can't begin to describe the helplessness my son and daughter-in-law experienced. Besides the physical illness of the pregnancy, my daughter-in-law had the additional worry and fear that her child may not survive to full term, or if she did survive that she would have to undergo a future surgery. For my wife and me, this diagnosis was very difficult as we waited each day and could only encourage and pray for a miracle.

The thing is, from all outward signs the pregnancy was progressing normally. Only a few people knew the stress the family was under. They endured weekly appointments with specialists, who used detailed imaging to monitor the lung mass and growth of the baby.

Then a miracle started to happen. After a few months doctors determined that the mass had stopped growing, and they were confident my granddaughter would most likely survive the gestation. Despite some initial problems during the high-risk delivery, she struggled but survived the birth.

After making it through the entire nine months, the child and family needed to overcome one more hurdle. They would need to wait three months for my granddaughter to grow large enough for surgeons to be able to remove the lower portion of her right lung. From outward appearance she was still a normal baby, yet the entire family knew there was a great physical challenge to overcome. This was truly a time when the family had to understand that the cure would require this trial path to get harder before it got better.

Skilled surgeons successfully removed the lower lobe of her right lung, but it was difficult for my son and daughter-in-law not to hold their child while she was in ICU (Intensive Care Unit) attached to so many tubes. Amazingly, the surgery was successful, and my granddaughter was home within four days.

Growth Actions: I can tell you now that growth was a word that struck fear into our family but also gave hope. When the doctors reported an unknown growth during a routine exam, it shocked all of us. Weekly, specialists measured the "growth" rate of the mass. Family members constantly prayed for my granddaughter to "grow" faster than the mass before she was born, and we were all excited when that actually happened. We then waited for three months after the delivery while she "grew" large enough to perform the surgery.

This young couple grew closer due to this trial. Our family grew closer due to my granddaughter's health challenge. My granddaughter may never remember this experience, but I know my son and daughter-in-law will never forget it. I know that it brought our family closer together, and we value every day we have with her.

TAP to Strong Growth: Although my granddaughter survived the surgery, the discovery that the mass in her lung was precancerous was very scary. Now that she has survived the surgery, she will undergo constant monitoring and have follow-up medical appointments for several years. Family and friends grew closer with this trial.

TAP to a Lifetime of Growth: This story explains that the signs and symptoms initially displayed to family and friends might indicate a deeper problem that still needs to be discovered. My granddaughter's story is still being written and is to be determined. We will all enjoy watching her grow both physically and emotionally.

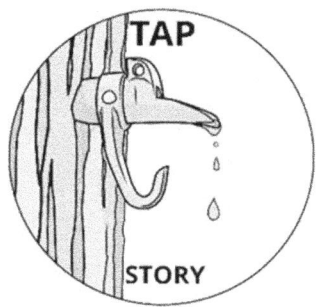

TAP Story: Stop Laughing, I Can't Breathe!
Main TAP Tool: Season of Symptoms
Low Point/Stress Point: No matter what I try I can't get air.

Trial Story: Have you ever struggled to catch your breath? Do you know anyone know with asthma or COPD (Chronic Obstructive Pulmonary Disease)? Perhaps you or someone you know has had pneumonia. Over the past few years, I have almost blacked out when I laughed too much.

I've struggled with breathing my entire life. As a child I struggled with breathing from time to time, and my parents would lay me on the floor in a bathroom and turn on a hot shower when I was having an attack to help me relax. Eventually I was diagnosed with asthma.

Despite my diagnosis, I'd always played sports growing up, such as soccer, baseball, and wrestling; all while I struggled with breathing and asthma. When I went to college, my symptoms became worse, especially during fall, winter, and spring seasons, because I struggled with allergies. I began to fear the seasons and made attempts to schedule my life events around them. Heaven forbid I developed a cold, as it seemed to exacerbate or increase my asthma symptoms.

During different times of the year, people close to me noticed that I had a breathing problem, struggled with asthma, and that I would have difficulty talking as the day progressed. Imagine constantly worrying about every breath you take, whether or not you would be able to complete a sentence, struggling to intake air and speak out loud, and almost passing out if I began to laugh too hard.

This has been my life. Most people think of me as being a very calm person during stressful situations, as I'm often soft spoken. In reality, it's the result of often having to hyper-focus on each breath I take. For the past twenty-five years I've been on a series of asthma-related medications, which include an entire regiment and use of rescue inhalers, oral steroids, peak flow meters, and nebulizers to help me with breathing treatments.

Over time my breathing seemed to get worse and worse, which required me to undergo breathing treatments in the morning when I got up. I have a portable breathing treatment nebulizer in my vehicle, and I would often take a couple breathing treatments while at work. I then had another breathing treatment before going home, another breathing treatment in the evening, and sometimes breathing treatments in the middle of night. It got so bad that while at a work training I started choking surrounded by all my co-workers. They were laughing and I started to black out. Somehow I was able to recover. Needless to say, breathing caused me a lot of problems.

In the course of my career, being in charge of so many treatment responsibilities required me to speak in public. Besides already being shy by nature, speaking always came with stress and worry that I would struggle to finish speaking. I also worried about being able to testify in court for a long period of time without coughing. It's affected my career and limited my abilities.

A few years ago, my wife decided to go to medical school and did a rotation with the local specialist dealing with allergies and vocal cord dysfunction. As I was getting no relief from all medications prescribed by my many doctors, my wife suggested that I make an appointment with the doctor she was working with to investigate my asthma.

Then something amazing happened. This doctor tried a new procedure. He actually tried to induce an asthma attack with a series of inhaled chemical irritants. I'm sure you're thinking the same thing I was at the time. "You're going to do what???" Reluctantly, I agreed to the test. Much to my surprise, and despite all their attempts to induce an asthma attack, I had no response to the chemicals. The doctor then used a camera scope to look at my vocal cords and found that, in fact, I had never had asthma. He did find that I suffer from a physical condition called Vocal Cord Dysfunction (VCD). Basically, when I take a deep breath to speak or laugh, instead of my vocal cords opening wide to take in oxygen, they try to close. It's the opposite of the way you want your body to respond to try to get a breath of air. If you want to experience my dilemma, try breathing and talking through a small straw at the same time. This new diagnosis blew my mind: I almost did not believe him.

Growth Actions: With this new understanding of the root cause of my breathing symptoms, my doctor ordered me to stop all my asthma medications and breathing treatments, which seemed contradictory to what I've been doing for so many years. I was sent to a vocal speech therapist for the second time in my life, as I had previously needed speech therapy as a child. Stopping my medications was easy, but with the initial treatment plan, I got much worse for a period of time. As an adult, speech therapy was a very humbling and sometimes humiliating experience to endure. The treatment included putting cameras in my nose and down the back of my throat to look at my vocal cords while I performed a series of speaking and singing assignments. Then it required a series of breathing and speaking exercises to teach me how to breathe and speak differently to retrain my vocal cords.

TAP to Strong Growth: As a middle-aged man, I had to pay extreme attention to every breath I was taking and to every word I was saying while being corrected constantly. After months of humiliating treatments, I began to get better control of my breathing. I can now proudly tell you -- three years later -- that I only struggle with breathing from time to time and only occasionally have relapses. Breathing exercises and meditation help prevent the relapses. I still take plenty of medications for other ailments such as cholesterol, but I've been asthma medicine-free for more than three years.

TAP to a Lifetime of Growth: I have shared this story with friends who had the same issues and one has also been diagnosed with VCD.

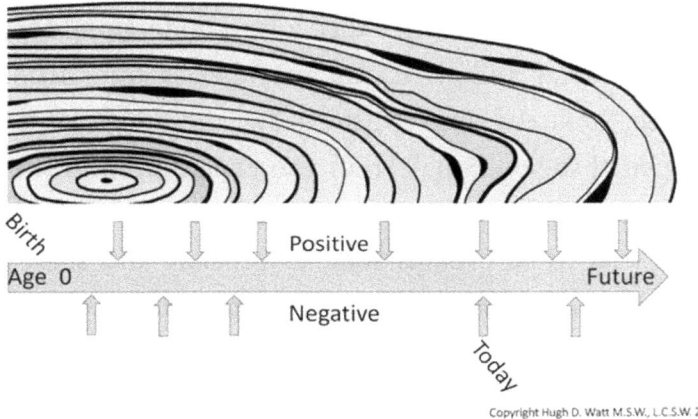

*"Each life will experience good and bad,
but identifying both will show the growth you have had."*

Counting the rings from the center outward will tell you how many years or seasons this tree has survived. Some rings will be very thin, and other rings will be very thick. Thin rings represent a normal or drought year for the tree's growth. A thick or fat ring represents a year of excessive water or above normal growth for the tree. At the bottom of this drawing is a timeline starting from birth and continuing into the future.

It is very difficult discover the tree's age and which years were good or bad unless the tree is cut down. When you are deep in a trial, you tend to see just that trial. It obscures your vision and blocks other things out. Step back and look at your life in total, not just this trial. Recognize that you have grown from past trials, and you will have more positive growth in your future.

As you go through life, you will experience many trials to help you grow. Sometimes it's difficult to understand the purpose of this trial and what you may be learning from the experience. You need time to heal, grow, and understand what has happened to you. Small trials you experienced in the past have helped you prepare for larger trials in the future. We often want the trial to be over as soon as possible and sometimes wonder why it is taking so long. Life lessons may not be understood until many years later or even until the end of our lives. Understand that growth comes from both positive and negative events in our lives.

This exercise will have you identify on the timeline the years in which good things happened to you and the years in which bad things happened. Examples might include the years you graduated high school, got married, got divorced, or lost a job. The point of this chart is to help you see that you have overcome trials in the past and might have even become stronger because of them.

Why You Need to Reframe Your Trials

Imagine what your life could be like if you reframed trials into something positive. What does reframe mean? It's kind of like looking for the positives in difficult situations. I realize that it may be impossible to find anything positive in your worst traumas but consider looking for something positive in the other trials you have faced. As an example, look at the drawings below. They show the same picture with different picture frames. The wood on one frame is warped and broken, barely holding the picture together. In the second frame the wood looks new and solid, and a floral pattern has been painted on it, beautifying the picture. A reframe is the process of looking at a trial as something you can grow from. It might be difficult or even impossible to imagine anything good coming from some trials such as abuse or cancer. I challenge you to find the growth beyond the trial. Be aware that it could take years to find any positives.

Trials Reframed

How I reframed poverty. I grew up in an atypical world as far as families are concerned. As I mentioned previously, my mother was raised in a semi-foster care family because her parents were somewhat neglectful, permissive, and had other dysfunctional issues. Her brothers, my uncles, were both entangled in the penal system.

My father lost his father to cancer when he was fifteen. He grew up being the man of the house with his two sisters, as his mom needed to go to work. He served in the military and then returned home and became a sheriff. From birth until age twelve, I did not see much of him as he worked graveyard shifts trying to provide for his young family.

Early in their marriage, my parents moved to a rural location in the middle of the California High Desert and attempted to provide for us. Although we lived far away from many of the conveniences of the city, we made do with our wide-open spaces. We lived on an acre and a half property and were surrounded by many acres of vacant desert properties. My dad made the best of the situation and found ways to attract kids from all around for me to associate with.

First, he installed a swimming pool. It was the only pool I knew of for many miles, and kids from all around came to take swimming lessons. Second, he rented a tractor to build a Bicycle Motocross (BMX) track on the back acre of our property, complete with a drop-off starting hill, berms, rollers, dips, and jumps. Third, he used the tractor to clear a go-kart track on the neighboring ten acres next to my house. Although I had endured teasing and bullying as a child, my parents made great efforts to help me have friends. I enjoyed all these comforts until I was twelve years old.

Needless to say, my mother's family being very "colorful" and my father being in law enforcement lead to many conflicts within our home. Their relationship always seemed strained, and it included some occasional separations. When I was twelve years old, my parents finally separated and eventually divorced three years later. Although divorce is common in law enforcement now, it was not very common at the time.

The divorce left us financially destitute, and soon all the open space and comforts I enjoyed were gone. The poverty was real, and my mother could no longer maintain the pool. It became an algae–infested, stagnant pond in the middle of the desert, which leaches, frogs, and ducks began to enjoy. The poverty became so bad that I still recall buying gifts for Christmas at garage sales and making my own board game pieces to complete missing sets for my brothers and sister. Our local church provided Christmas gifts for us during the holiday. I went from being taken care of by parents to being on the free lunch program in school.

My mother began dating again and remarried a man eleven years younger than herself who was still in his twenties and working for his dad's concrete company. Being poor was bad, but it was about to get a lot worse.

My mother and stepfather decided to move us out of our town and away from all my friends into a home that we shared with a lady we did not know. We stayed there for a few months, and then we moved into a two-bedroom apartment, where my younger brother, sister and I shared a single bedroom. Sharing a room with my brother and sister was an adjustment, but it was nothing compared to the next trial that would soon come.

My mother and stepfather eventually purchased an empty property on which they hoped to build a new home. In order to save money to purchase supplies to build the home, we moved into two small camping trailers at the back of the empty lot. (See the photos below). Although sharing a bedroom was challenging, moving us three kids into a very small trailer was beyond embarrassing. For the next two and a half years we lived in these trailers and used an outhouse. I was so embarrassed that I tried to hide the circumstances of my life from my high school friends. Image how my life had changed. Image going from a life of growing up with parents, having a stable income, a swimming pool, go-karts, BMX track, and many friends, to living in borrowed trailers, washing clothes in laundromats, using outhouses, and trying to make new friends. This marriage also eventually ended in another divorce for my mother.

Poverty Reframed

Although my life had many challenges, I have reframed these experiences for the better. I have reframed this near-homeless living from being the most embarrassing time in my life to what motivated both my siblings and me to work multiple jobs throughout our lives to ensure we would never end up this poor again. Now we teach our children that we can overcome hard things if we stick together as a family.

I could not control my parents' arguing and eventual divorce. I could not control my poverty. I could not control my living situation. I could not control others that bullied me. I could not control my growth height. All I could control was my attitude, my attendance in school, my participation in sports, my choice in friends, and my decisions to avoid criminal activity and drugs.

If you have worried in the past that you just can't overcome your specific trial, I want to put those fears to rest. You might not be able to do this with all trials, but you can do this with many of them. I have helped thousands of others succeed with all sorts of trials. Sometimes it just takes the right person with the ability to help you reframe your trials to explain it to you in a simple, understandable way.

Here is another reframe idea. How powerful is a word? What do you think of when you hear these words: mental, illness, disorder, diagnosis, anxiety, Post- Traumatic Stress Disorder (PTSD), mood disorders, depression, addiction, sadness, addict, shame, or trauma? We should attempt to use words that are less stigmatizing or that have less of a negative label.

The words we use are powerful. Consider reframing the meaning you place on the following:

Why is the word "post" used by therapists, for example, PTSD? Some professionals use the word "post" instead of using the word "after." It's like saying, "After the trial occurred," you're going to have some stress, anxiety, depression, reoccurring memories, and grief.

If you're given any label or diagnosis, decide to change your internal definition.

I want you to reframe any systemic label given to you after a trial. Don't think of it as something wrong with you. What you are experiencing is typical. I help others like you by reframing the symptoms or diagnosis. For example:

- You have been told you have an anxiety "disorder"? This trial can lead to growth from the anxiety.
- You have a depressive "disorder"? This can lead to growth from the depression.
- You have PTSD? Although this is more difficult than most disorders, it is an opportunity for a new reframe. This can lead to growth after the trauma.
- Never refer to yourself again as having PTSD, but now say, "I'm experiencing or have experienced, Post-traumatic Stress and Growth (PTSG).
- Remember: a person that used to abuse drugs or alcohol is not "clean," but is in recovery.
- You are a victim? No, you are a survivor!

In the current culture where everyone is sensitive to what people or groups are called, it is amazing to me that we still use the word "disorder." It sounds like there is something wrong with you. I want you to reframe this word "disorder." The goal is not to identify with the symptom or diagnosis. In other words, I'm not an alcoholic; I'm a person who struggles with alcoholism.

TRIAL TAPPERS

I have been involved with a specialized court for those struggling with lifelong illnesses like schizophrenia. A few years ago, I recommended that we change the name from Mental Health Court to Behavioral Health Court. The word "mental" has too many negative connections. The change was made, and many clients and staff appreciated the reframing of this one word. Perhaps someday the National Alliance on Mental Illness (NAMI) will change their name to the National Alliance on Behavioral Illnesses (NABI).

When you experience trials, it's typical for you to have occasional sadness, anxiety, and possibly depression. Some difficult traumas like abuse or death of a close family member or friend may take time to overcome, and you may need to seek help from professionals in order to grow like I did after my brother's death.

Let me try to explain it in another way. When your car starts to act differently, you will probably take it to a mechanic and try to explain what you think is wrong. After listening to your best guess, the mechanic will try to diagnose the problem by listening and running some diagnostic tests. What does the diagnosis mean besides a big bill? Something went wrong with one part of the car. The entire car is not broken, just one part that affects the rest of its performance. The mechanic will make adjustments and repairs to some very specific parts, and after a little time it may even run better than it did before.

When you go to the doctor, they will attempt to diagnose your medical condition based on the symptoms you share with the doctor and what they see after running tests. Once the problem is properly diagnosed, they can recommend very specific treatments for that problem.

Let me simply explain what could happen when you seek professional help while experiencing a more difficult life trial.

When you go to a therapist, like me, we will also try to "diagnose" your mental health "illness" or "condition." We will listen to your symptoms, ask you questions, and possibly have you answer written tests. Eventually we will come up with a diagnosis and tell you we found the problem: you have some "disorder." For example: depression, anxiety disorder.

Disorder??? Sounds bad, right? What a ridiculous word! Who wants to brag about this to your friends? Will this increase your status on Facebook or with your friends and coworkers? Having your condition labeled as a "disorder" can add to your anxiety, stress, and depression. You probably already feel bad about your life trial, and now a professional has confirmed there is something wrong with you because you have a "disorder." In simple terms, professionals use the word "disorder" to explain a pattern of negative reactions a person is experiencing for a significant amount of time which causes distress in their life. This usually affects their patterns of behaviors, thoughts, and feelings after a difficult trauma.

Everyone will experience symptoms or reactions of anxiety, stress and, dare I say, depression from time to time. Some trials only make you sad temporarily, but other severe traumas can cause even the strongest people to have reactions that require professional help.

You are not alone. Just look up what NAMI reports:

- Approximately one in five adults in the U.S. (46.6 million) experiences mental illness in a given year.[1]
- Approximately one in twenty-five adults in the U.S. (11.2 million) experiences a serious mental illness in a given year that substantially interferes with or limits one or more major life activities.[2]
- About 6.9 percent of adults in the U.S. (16 million) had at least one major depressive episode in the past year.[3]
- About 18.1 percent of adults in the U.S. experienced an anxiety disorder such as PTSD, obsessive-compulsive disorder, and specific phobias.[4]
- Among the 20.2 million adults in the U.S. who experienced a substance use disorder, 50.5 percent (10.2 million) had a co-occurring mental illness.[5]

If you seek professional help and are given a diagnosis, consider this a positive path to accelerated growth. Many people around you are experiencing similar trials, yet too many resist the help, suffer longer than needed, and fail to grow from the trial. Why do they suffer alone? Because of fear and possibly this one word "disorder" and how those less informed define it. If you find yourself experiencing more negative reactions than you can deal with, I hope you will be wise -- and ask for help.

As you read this book and answer questions, you should attempt to reframe your trials. Look at trials from a different perspective. In the simplest form, for example, I would reframe being laid off from a job as an opportunity to find a better job. In the most difficult form, I would reframe my brother's suicide as something I will use to help others.

I had plenty of life's experiences to bring me to my eventual profession of social worker. I chose to break the generational life cycle and surpass the education levels of any family members by going to college to become a social worker.

It is ironic that my career eventually resulted in me going to prison. Not as an inmate, but as a therapist running the largest drug program in the State of Utah. For more than twenty years I've worked with clients dealing with many different trials, such as domestic violence, sexual abuse, sexual addictions, substance abuse addictions, self-harm, marital problems, financial problems, suicide, depression, mental illness, plus many more.

Often the trial we are experiencing seems to dominate all our thoughts, emotions, and feelings during the crisis. This flood of emotions can give us a very narrow perspective on our entire life. Your life is more than a few trials. You must identify both trials and successes in your life. The following exercise will help you see a new perspective on your trials. Some trials might actually have been positive as you look back at them over time. How is this possible? Five years ago the loss of my wife's business felt like a huge financial and personal trial. Now that she has gone back to school and become a medical Physician's Assistant (PA), she would identify this trial as both bad and good.

Some trials you originally believed were negative might now be labeled as something positive in your life. Read the stories below and answer the questions in this exercise to help you see that you have already overcome trials and that there are many positive things to come when looking forward.

I wish we could all see the impact we have on those around us. I wish my brother Cody could have looked past the bad day he was having and seen all those whose lives he impacted while he was alive. I was amazed at all the people who came to his funeral and expressed positive things about him. Although he was struggling with many trials in life, he made a great impact on many people.

I challenge you to answer the following questions to help you identify your symptoms so you can dig deeper into the root of your problem in future chapters.

The health of a tree often appears in the leaves. Unhealthy signs and symptoms such as lack of water or nutrients will be manifested in the leaves, but often the cause can be found hidden deep in the roots. Sometimes the symptoms we exhibit, such as anxiety, depression, addictions, or self-harm, can be predicted based on when you experienced the trial; for example, losing a family member around a certain holiday. Reoccurring and/or increasing symptoms need to be addressed by pinpointing the negative life event that is associated with the holiday or season. Identify the seasons when you have internal difficulties.

1. Identify the seasons when you have internal difficulties.

2. What are the symptoms?

3. Identify which season is the worst for you.

4. What helps you endure until the season changes?

5. Who will you talk to about your worst seasons and how they can help you make it to the next?

Often when you are going through a trial you might try to address a symptom, but until you get to the root of the problem, you will make little lasting progress. It is important to dig deep and address the true reason why some behaviors are occurring. One way of changing your perspective on your past is to look back on your trials and recognize, not just the pain they caused, but also recognize the positive growth and change that occurred.

This is your chance to look back on your entire life, not just the current trial you are experiencing. Complete your own *Life Growth Timeline* by answering the questions below. You may have to return to this section often as you read and recall the positive things that have happened in your life.
Complete your *Life Growth Timeline* exercise by filling in the timeline below.

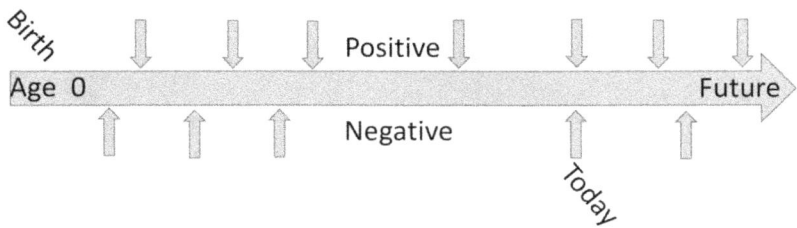

Timeline Questions:

Mark above the timeline all the good things that have happened in your life.

Mark below the timeline the trials that have happened in your life.

1. What good and bad effects do storms have on a tree?

    Good:

    Bad:

2. Mark below the timeline two challenges you are planning for in the future.

3. Mark above the timeline five positive things you are planning for in the future.

4. How does listing both the trials and successes on the timeline below change your view for the future in a positive way?

5. Which previous trials below are now good things in your life?

Internalization: Help Someone – Go and Teach Someone this Life Tap.

Record your thoughts...

_____
_____
_____

Record what you are grateful for...
_____
_____
_____

Record your commitment to positive action...
_____
_____
_____

Recap: Anniversaries, birthdays, or holidays can be difficult reminders of particular trials. Treat the real problem, not just the symptoms. Many trials can be reframed from negative to positive experiences with the passing of time. Identify, not only the trials you may have faced, but also the positive things you have and will experience in life.

As a Trial Tapper I admit when I'm sad and going through trials.

• CHAPTER 4 •

TAP #3: Tap Your Helpful Others – Family OR Friends!

"Others can help you during life's trials, and you will help others during theirs."

TAP Overview: This TAP illustrates that you will probably need the help of others to overcome some of your trials. This includes both those who have experienced your particular trial, as well as those who have not. Identify those you know who are willing to help and those you do not know, such as support groups or therapists, etc. Who can you help in the future?

The next visual lesson is called *Tap Your Helpful Others* during trials. The image is of a tapped maple tree with sap dripping out. A pair of hands is holding a galvanized metal bucket against the maple tree and under a metal tap to collect the dripping sap.

I use this exercise when working with clients who are experiencing trials in life. It is a brainstorming technique to help them acknowledge and identify the people around them who are willing to help. These might be friends from the past, current family or friends, or even people in their community they don't know well. I try to help them identify three friends, plus one therapist, one spiritual guide, and people such as volunteers and first responders, medical professionals, firemen, and police.

The key is for you to make a list of your own. My guess is that you will fail to list some important people. This TAP exercise will help you develop that list of *Helpful Others* without adding more stress to your current situation.

It is not uncommon for an inexperienced—or even an experienced—therapist or probation officer to create goals for you without your input. For example, one goal might be to visit your family every week. This might look great on paper; however, you are the only one who knows whether your family will be helpful or hurtful during this time. If your family has been physically or emotionally abusive, you might need to avoid them for now. Another example would be if you are currently experiencing a trial of unemployment, and someone recommends you ask a former employer for employment. This could be a good idea unless you left that employer due to harassment from the boss.

Be careful who you ask for help. Often when we experience a trial in life, society tells us to "suck it up." It will get better with time. Why do some people give you the cold shoulder when you are at your lowest point? I think some just don't know what to say or do. Do people unintentionally tell others to "suck it up"? It happens all the time. This actually happened to me.

After my brother's death, I called my insurance company to ask about coverages for therapy. The customer service worker asked some questions about my problem, and I told him I was having challenges in my relationship during this time of grief. He told me my sessions might not be covered. He said, "We won't pay for things like couples therapy just to make you feel happy in your marriage. You need to be diagnosed with something more serious." There it was. I needed a "disorder" diagnosis.

If you or others feel you are not managing to "deal with it," you may consider seeing a therapist. As a Licensed Clinical Social Worker (LCSW), I know some great therapists. Yet if we professionals are honest with ourselves, we will acknowledge that some therapists may not listen to your needs or provide the correct tools for your success.

When you start therapy, your therapist will have to create a plan for your treatment which will help you and which will also be acceptable to your insurances company. I have been auditing therapists and reviewing their "treatment plans" across my state for years. It is all too common that those seeking help have never seen the "plan" or agreed with the "goals" that are outlined in it. During these audits, many professionals have difficulty explaining to me, a peer, let alone their clients, how they can actually help with a client's trials. Some therapists act like they are all knowledgeable about their client's success. All too often I see the same goals and plans for multiple clients. Some therapists fail, not only to show clients the plan, but also fail to teach them how to apply skills during future trials. Thus the client needs to return for help each time they have new major trial in life.

Sometimes the "system" is stacked against you. Insurance companies may not want to pay for treatment. Costly copays might prevent you from going to a doctor or therapist. When I showed up to therapy saying I was having difficulty "adjusting" to my brother's death, one therapist regrettably said, "Most insurances won't pay for adjustment disorders. They want something more serious like anxiety, depression, or PTSD."

Although not all trials you face will necessitate seeing a doctor or therapist, I do believe there are times when you will need one or both. You are not helpless in your search for the right providers, and once you find them, you need to be willing to do more than just listen to their advice. You will have to do the homework such as journaling or taking medications. The right helpers can be invaluable to your success.

Be selective in your choice. Some doctors and therapists might only focus on your symptoms, and some may be actually practicing on you. They are taking a shot in the dark when they attempt to relieve your symptoms. Doctors and therapists are required to document very specific treatment goals and plans for your recovery. They must document goals in order to bill insurance plans and to get paid. You have the right to know your plan and should ask for it. Open your mouth. Be demanding. Be informed about your plan and ask questions.

What do you want to focus on? When I decided I needed additional help from a professional, I knew I wanted to address specific problems: adjusting to my brother's death and the events at the funeral. I knew I wanted a trauma-informed therapist to do Eye Movement Desensitization and Reprocessing (EMDR) Therapy with me. I had a direction and goals of my own. Don't waste your time and money trying to work on things you don't want to focus on. Make suggestions about what you want to see happen. Sometimes you don't know what's wrong and need to explore your life with the help of a guide, but often you do know what's wrong and just need help finding solutions. Be very active in identifying what you want help with. Be honest and tell your therapist what you like and dislike. You should have constant input into your treatment plan and understand the goals.

When I was looking for my therapist I didn't just accept the first therapist that took my insurance or that was now accepting patients. I looked them up on-line and reviewed their credentials. I asked them questions and interviewed them by phone, text, or email. I asked very specific questions: How long have they been in practice? How many clients have they worked with who had my background or specific problem? What was their gender? You may ask why gender makes a difference.

Some victims of abuse don't want a therapist who is the same gender of their abuser. In other words, does the therapist understand the physical, social, and emotional impact of trauma on the individual? What approach do they use to treat trauma?

Everyone will experience trauma at some time in their lives, and most of the time you will not need formal intervention. But when a person does need additional help, understand that asking for help is a major leap forward on the path to growth.

Sometimes your first attempt at finding a therapist may not work out because you may feel more comfortable with therapists of a specific gender, age, or religious belief. Finding a good therapist can help you overcome your trials and especially your traumas, but you should feel comfortable asking for specific plans to achieve your goals. The TAPs in this book will help you overcome many of the trials on your own and help you identify any specific areas you might need help from a professional.

How will you know if you need to see a professional? If you have one very traumatic event or trial, the need for a professional might seem obvious. Other times trials just build up and overwhelm us. Again, not everyone will need to see a professional for every trial, but if you are having some of these reactions or responses, it's something you should consider. For example, if you have been experiencing the following reactions for more than a month: anxiety, anger, daydreaming, nightmares, change in eating habits, excessive alcohol intake, risk taking, difficulty making decisions, high level of fear, diminished hygiene, self-medicating, violence, depression, panic attacks, guilt, hallucinations, and/or trouble sleeping. This is not an exhaustive list of every possible indicator that you need more help, but you get the idea. Now to be absolutely clear: If you are having feelings of helplessness, hopelessness, extreme guilt, and suicidal thoughts for any amount of time, you need help immediately. CALL 911.

As a Trial Tapper you are more aware of the growth opportunities professionals can bring and choose this path when needed.

Finding positive and *Helpful Others* will take a little bit of effort, but I encourage you not to give up. If you feel you have no positive friends in your life, then you may need to develop positive friends by reconnecting with former high school classmates, taking up a new hobby, or attending a religious group.

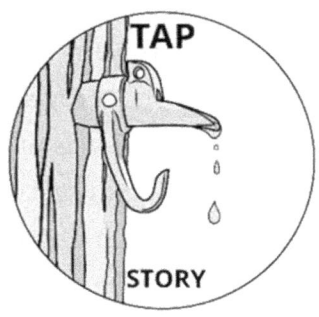

Trial TAP: Con-Quest
Main TAP Tool: Helpful Others
Low Point/Stress Point: You're in charge of the program.
TAP Story: There I was, just a few years out of graduate school, when I was offered a job as a therapist in a 144-bed resi-

dential substance abuse program called Con-Quest, which was inside a state prison. This was a newly formed federal grant program that was attempting to provide treatment for inmates. And the big thing was, at the time I entered the program I found that it was really struggling to provide structure and accountability for all involved.

I found that gang leaders, who had no intention of changing, had moved into the program. More drugs could be found inside the program than in the rest of the prison. Most officers overseeing the program considered the program a joke or failure, because many of the inmates had not made any progress in the entire three years it had been in place and because the program staff was not reliable. It was not uncommon for the counselors or therapists to show up late to work, cancel group sessions without notice, leave work early, and refuse to participate in any "security" functions.

Growth Actions: The big problem was that within a few months of my arrival the second program director in three years was suddenly removed, and I was offered the position of directing this failing attempt at drug treatment within the prison walls. That meant the federal grant program was in jeopardy of failing and unlikely to be continued when the allotted five years was up. This led me to fear that being successful in the job was impossible, that I too would soon be replaced. Needless to say, I was stressed out. I don't know if I was too naive to know what I had just taken on. Can you see how I might have felt overwhelmed?

TAP to Strong Growth: The title of "Director" did not give me all the knowledge I needed to fix this program. Then I got a lucky break. Something amazing happened. Someone had found training money in the budget, and I had the opportunity to visit three successful drug programs in California prisons. This trip was so valuable, and instantly it became crystal clear to me how I needed my program to change. When I returned from this trip, I began a campaign to implement a series of drastic changes. My plan was to start transforming our "program" into a Therapeutic Community (TC) following the models I had seen, with the help of trainers from the National Institute of Corrections.

So I started by first requiring the professional staff to demonstrate higher standards by following a dress code, showing up to work on time, and apologizing to both security staff and inmates when they failed to follow through with their responsibilities. The professional staff was also required to assist the security staff during stressful times such as prison-wide lockdowns and inmate or cell searches. We consulted with and listened to the security staff about what we needed to do to maintain safety while providing treatment.

But I didn't stop there. Second, I implemented a series of cardinal rules for participating in the program and held a zero tolerance for drug use and violence while in the program. I then required strict adherence in attending classes and groups and tracked the progress or lack thereof.

Third, I campaigned for the administration to help me change the physical appearance of the cell blocks to promote a culture of change. These changes included changing the color of the paint and allowing positive slogans and murals to be painted in the prison sections.

Because Con-Quest was not respected by inmates or staff, the decision to implement positive changes to create a culture of accountability was not received well by either group. Over the next few months I had to remove many inmates from the program, and most of the staff requested transfers or quit rather than agreeing to be held accountable for their own actions. With so much internal change happening, the security staff placed actual bets on how long I would last as the third and possibly last Program Director.

TAP to a Lifetime of Growth: After most of my staff quit, I had to get creative. How do you run a full-time program when all the staff you supervise quit? You need a clear vision of the possibilities. I had a vision of what Con-Quest could become. I wrote a five-year plan with very specific goals that culminated in securing a stand-alone facility outside the general prison population to accommodate 400 residents.

With all the staff quitting and 144 inmates needing to attend classes, I became an adjunct professor at a major university and recruited fifty interns majoring in education to assist me in teaching the twenty-four classes until we could hire enough staff that agreed with my vision.

At first, change was slow. It took persistence to help the security staff understand that our professional staff was responsible, and that both they and the inmates participating in the program could change.

The positive changes gained momentum over the next few years. Building on each success got easier, and we were having positive results. Within my five years as Program Director, our team was able to achieve most, if not all, of our goals, and we were able to expand into a 400-bed stand-alone facility. When we began the process of staffing, the facility security staff no longer made any bets about how long I would last and instead were requesting to join me in my efforts.

The success achieved by my team in implementing the TC led to me training and mentoring several local jails as they developed their own programs. Prior to my leaving to work in the federal system, I received the prestigious Director's Achievement Award from the Department of Corrections. The award in part states, "He was a key player in the development of Therapeutic Communities in the Department... Through his efforts, Hugh transformed a struggling program into one that has less than 30 percent recidivism."

This is an example of a positive story that can demonstrate the journey anyone can take and apply to his/her own life. I could never have done this alone. It took the help of students, co-workers, administrators, security personnel, and even the inmates themselves. Everyone was a *Helpful Other*. Any success and awards I received was a direct result of seeking help from others.

Positive peer support, in conjunction with therapy, can aid your recovery. As the former director of Con-Quest, a 400-bed residential drug program in the Utah State Prison, I was certified several times in the Therapeutic Community or "TC" model to help people dealing with addictions. I am a big believer in the TC and the impact of peer support, in combination with therapy, to further your recovery. Being surrounded by positive peers working to improve your community and guided by a therapist can have positive outcomes.

Why do I believe you may need a therapist in combination with positive peer supports? Because often I find the symptoms being displayed by clients, such as addiction or harmful behaviors, are a result of past unresolved traumas. As explained in the beginning of this book, everyone should be trauma aware or trauma informed. If you rely only on positive peers to overcome some trials, you may begin to feel a little better, but you may never actually resolve the underlying cause of your symptoms.

Being the treatment and contracting specialist for all therapy for federal felons coming out of prison in the State of Utah gives me the opportunity to audit and investigate many different treatment programs. For the most part, programs I encounter are very helpful, and many hire a combination of both peers and professionals. Occasionally, however, I will come across a program that is anti-therapist. And if a therapist is required by state licensing, it only hires therapists that have experienced the same problem as the clients, such as recovering addicts. Some programs only focus on hard work, accountability, and their impact on the community in order to help clients focus on others instead of themselves. Some of these programs not only discount therapists but refuse any clients that are taking psychotropic medications for such elements as anxiety or depression. Programs that refuse to use therapists, and possibly medications, to help clients to deal with past traumas may overlook the main reason their client experiences symptoms of anxiety and depression. Volunteer support groups and peers are often helpful, but it is very common that you will need the help of a professional therapist to process some of the worst trials you face.

A few program directors and their clients have told me things such as, "You can't help an addict unless you have been an addict," "You can't help someone who has been raped unless you have been raped." "You can't understand what I'm going through because you never went through it yourself." "You should not treat an addiction to illegal drugs by replacing it with another legal drug." These statements and arguments are sometimes compelling, yet I believe this line of thinking is flawed.

The key is to not rule out anyone who wants to help. There is a huge group of individuals who volunteer to help people during trials. These volunteers are often called peer supports, addiction recovery sponsors, support groups, etc. Often people find help because they feel a connection to someone who has experienced a similar trial as themselves. Although a trained therapist, I am also a certified peer support for law enforcement officers experiencing a trial or trauma. It is natural for people to feel more comfortable talking to someone who could be considered their peer.

The more life experiences one has, the more they can assist others who are struggling during trials in life. For example, having been married for more than twenty-six years, as a therapist I have the credibility to help someone with marriage trials. I ask you to attempt to help others dealing with similar trials mentioned throughout this book. It's common for people who are struggling to want help from others who have been through similar challenges. As I outline in this book, I struggled in school, was bullied, lived in poverty, raised three boys, had financial setbacks, had my brother commit suicide, and had been in therapy myself. My life experiences give me empathy for others enduring similar trials, but they are not a requirement for me to help others with their individual trials. You may seek *Helpful Others* with similar trials, but there are many friends and professionals who can help you grow and recover even though they have not been through your exact trial. Therapists are not required to have experienced your trial in order to help you, and asking for such a therapist may limit your options.

Over my career I have helped hundreds of people who have beaten their spouses, yet I have never hit my spouse. I have worked with many men that are sex offenders, yet I have never acted out sexually against anyone. I have helped thousands of men and women recover from addictions, yet I have never been addicted to any illegal drugs. I believe in peer support and the value of someone experiencing similar pasts, yet I also believe in the value of trained therapists and physicians to help you understand the root of your trials.

I do not have a medical degree, but I encourage my clients to visit their physician. My wife is a PA working for a family practice clinic. She often treats individuals seeking help for depression or anxiety and who are in need of medications. A standard practice is for her to recommend and order blood labs, and sometimes she discovers that her patients are lacking different nutrients which are causing chemical imbalances that must be addressed.

Those suffering from depression, who refuse to recognize that their symptoms might be caused by a medical issue, are similar to diabetics who refuse to recognize they need insulin to regulate their blood sugar levels. I am a strong believer in treating people with both therapy and medical interventions. My wife is a wise medical provider who often prescribes medications to address symptoms of anxiety and depression and also prescribes a therapist for counseling.

I enlist a variety of people to help me with my trials. I can always call on family, friends, coworkers, and a large religious group for help. When I first learned that my brother had gone missing, my family enlisted help from anyone who was willing to help—not just those who had a suicidal family member. We found help from family, friends, rescue volunteers, and strangers. After more than twenty-four hours of searching we found my brother. In the following days church leaders, coworkers, and many other people also stepped forward to help, including many that never had a family member commit suicide.

One of my *Helpful Others* is Jason Webb. We are as close as brothers even though we have different mothers. We began our friendship while studying in the city of Jerusalem as young adults. We then became college roommates, and for the past twenty-six years our families have been close, and we get together often. I would do anything to help Jason and his family, and he would do the same for me.

Another *Helpful Other* in my life is Dave Murray. We've spent many hours and nights together working to refine our skills in helping people learn to overcome personal trials. We have worked together within the prison system evaluating new materials and new activities geared to help people who are at their lowest point grow stronger. We have spent many weekend nights at my house working and just spending time together as friends. He has truly been a friend on whom I can always count.

Rick Delray is another *Helpful Other*. Rick was my former field partner prior to him transferring to take over the supervision of all federal felons on three of the Hawaiian Islands. Rick and I started our career about the same time and had the same desires to help people struggling with internal challenges.

Another *Helpful Other* in my life is Greg Petersen, my coworker and field partner most of the time. We are together in the same car up to twelve hours a day. Our lives are literally in each other's hands; we would defend each other against any threat to the death. Our time together has created a friendship in which we support each other through the trials we face in life. We truly share the highs and lows of our lives together, both professional and personal. I learned some great advice from his wife Karen when their family was experiencing a difficult time. She said, "I will never ask someone experiencing a trial the following: How can I help? What can I do for you? Call me if you need something. During a crisis, it's best if you do kind acts of service without being asked." Find nice things to do for others that are struggling. If you feel like taking cookies to someone, then do it. Have dinner delivered, take care of their pet, shovel the snow, or mow the grass. I promise you will be happier if you serve others.

I have personally found help with my biggest trials, the death of my brother and the abuse as a child, by working with several different professional *Helpful Others*. One very helpful treatment I have participated in is EMDR Therapy . This treatment "uses a patient's own rapid, rhythmic eye movements to dampen the power of emotionally charged memories of past traumatic events."[4] This treatment approach has been found to be very effective in helping people cope with the most painful traumas and memories in their life. It just made sense to me, as it addresses many of the same learning styles I addressed in the introduction of this book.

This therapy is combined with directed eye movements, hand-tapping, and audio stimulation. It has been found to be very effective with victims and especially veterans and first responders who have experienced trauma. EMDR enables you to heal from the symptoms of emotional distress. Your body naturally heals itself from many physical wounds, and the tools used in EMDR help your brain naturally reprocess disturbing events to rapidly help emotional healing begin. I did therapy using all three techniques, visual, audio, and handheld electronic buzzers or tappers. The benefits of EMDR are well-researched, and I

---

[4] WebMD, EMDR: Eye Movement Desensitization and Reprocessing

would encourage you to find an EMDR-certified therapist to address your unresolved or lingering traumas or trials. Go to www.emdr.com to find a certified therapist near you.

Who are your *Helpful Others*? This TAP will help you identify those family, friends, coworkers, therapists, doctors, volunteers, etc., that can support you during your trial. If you have difficulty answering the question, "Who are your three positive friends?" You might connect with former high school friends on social media. Also, you can always find online support groups for any trial you face.

Service animals or pets can be included as additional *Helpful Others*. There is plenty of research explaining how animals will help improve your mood. Many military veterans are being paired with service dogs to help lift their spirits and overcome their trials. Over the last several years my family has had three different dogs, and all have had a great impact on my family.

A couple of years ago my son and I picked up our current dog, Charlie, from the pound. He is a Labrador/Pit Bull mix that was tied to a tree in a park and abandoned. Charlie is a very mean-looking animal, yet his disposition is like a very needy puppy. It's amazing to watch this strong, big dog patiently let my grandchildren play on top of him as they cover him with towels. Charlie cheers me up when I come home from a long day. He is always there to greet me at the door, waiting to go outside to play ball. He follows me everywhere I go in the house. He sits next to me to watch television and waits outside my room while I change clothing.

Most of this book has been written with Charlie by my side, or at least sleeping near me. If you're feeling down or depressed due to your trials, consider getting an animal that you can pet. Some researchers claim petting animals will lower your blood pressure and brighten your mood. If you can't take on the responsibility of a pet at this time, go visit your local animal shelter and volunteer to take care of the lost animals there.

To be clear, you may need different levels of *Helpful Others*, depending on the specific trial or trauma and your reactions to each. The help might come from one or all of the following: talking to a friend or family member, meeting with a spiritual leader, getting input from a peer, attending an organized support group, and/or talking to a professional.

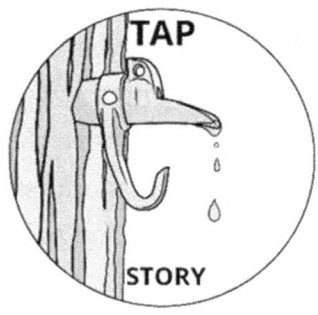

TAP Story: Kind Woman Becomes a *Helpful Other*
Main TAP Tool: Helpful Others
Low Point/Stress Point: "I'm praying for you to find your son."

Trial Story: There we were, waiting to hear anything from Search and Rescue about my brother whom we believed was in a mountain valley. Our family hoped for the best, but as the hours went on my mother became increasingly worried. We were accepting help from anyone that would show up to help search. Some of the search members who helped my family had been through similar situations, but they were now at a point in life where they could reach out and help us. I recall the time we that we were comforted as we waited for news. One kind woman, who lived in a home near the foothills, offered our family the use of her home from time to time for breaks.

Growth Actions: This kind woman did more than allow us to use her house. Coincidentally, she had previously lost a child of her own. Now, years later, she had the strength to console and cry with my mother as we discovered my brother had taken his life. Instantly we bonded with this perfect stranger.

TAP to Strong Growth: How did this woman get past the loss of her own child to the point of being able to help my grieving mother? Who helped her along the way in her own journey of healing? I'm sure she had to survive the same holidays and anniversaries we all had to endure months after the funeral.

TAP to a Lifetime of Growth: The pain is too great for my mother at this time to possibly help others, yet with time I'm sure she too will be able to help a grieving mother in the future.

Maple trees need help to turn the water into something better. There are people all around us willing to help turn trials and pain into something better. There is strength in asking for help.

1. When have you helped someone experiencing a trial in life?

2. What did you do to help them?

3. What activities can others help you with during your next trial?

4. List three people you will educate on what works to help you during a trial.

5. List five people you don't personally know but would help you with a trial in life.

Internalization: Help Someone – Go and Teach Someone this Life Tap.

Record your thoughts...
_____
_____
_____

Record what you are grateful for...
_____
_____
_____

Record your commitment to positive action...
_____
_____
_____

Recap: Most of us will need the help of others to overcome some trials. People that have experienced your particular trial can be helpful, as well as others who have not. Identify those you know willing to help and those you do not know. Who can you help?

As a Trial Tapper I humble myself to accept help from others, including therapists and doctors, during the most difficult traumas.

• CHAPTER 5 •

TAP #4: Tap Your Unseen Power to Overcome Trials – Bigger than Yourself!

"External power can be challenged during any trial, yet overcoming all trials can increase your internal power."

TAP Overview: This TAP will help you understand that sometimes your only help will come from your *Unseen Power*. You may decide to grow towards this power, or you may pull away during trials. Forgiveness is debatable and is not required for your growth, but it may help.

This visual example is *Tap Your Unseen Power to Overcome Trials*. Imagine an on and off switch next to a huge electrical plug. Above and below the switches and the plug are various symbols depicting religious groups, nature, and meditation. When I moved into a previously owned home, I was initially excited to find a 220-volt plug in my garage, which I expected to use for an air compressor or a welder. I soon found out that the previous owner of the home had actually wired a 110-volt into 220-volt plug.

This deceptively wired plug is a perfect lesson to teach about an *Unseen Power* many turn to during their trials. This *Unseen Power* is sometimes referred to as a God, spirituality, religion, meditation, nature, or the universe. You cannot see the strength and power of this "power plug" to which you alone control the on and off switch.

During my life I have studied various religions. In my twenties I lived for twenty months in northern Brazil as a missionary. I also spent over three months in Jerusalem, a city which is sacred to a number of religions and traditions. While there I was exposed to many different faiths. I had the opportunity to study Islam, Judaism, and Christianity in-depth under the tutelage of several prestigious religious leaders including George Pace, Truman and Ann Madsen, Rabbi David Rosen, and Nafez Nazzal. I also visited many religious sites in Israel and Egypt while studying the Bible, the Torah, and the Quran.

While living in these different countries, I found that many people profess a connection to an *Unseen Power*. The internal intensity of that connection and power varies greatly and is distinctive for different people. In fact, my own family is made up of strong believers in Catholicism, Greek Orthodox, The Church of Jesus Christ of Latter-day Saints, Buddhism, and atheism.

Many people I've worked with connect to one or more of these *Unseen Powers*. Even those who do not profess to believe in an organized religion will often acknowledge some *Unseen Power* that keeps the planets and stars in motion in the universe. During extreme trials some people struggle with their understanding of this *Unseen Power* while others grow in trust and turn on their power switch to access this *Unseen Power* for greater strength and support. Their connection to the *Unseen Power* increases because of their trial. I caution those I work with from taking extreme positions towards or against an *Unseen Power* right after a big trial or trauma.

Trials and traumas can challenge the strength of their belief in an *Unseen Power* for many. They lose faith or have a decrease in their previously held support of an *Unseen Power* and might even turn their switches off. They begin to believe there is no *Unseen Power* in the universe or feel their *Unseen Power* let this trial happen to them despite all the good they had done in life.

Sometimes your trauma or trial may be so devastating that *Helpful Others* can only do so much to relieve your pain. When this happens, I encourage you to find whatever *Unseen Power* you can rely on to bring you peace once again. It's not uncommon for someone's outer appearance to suggest that they are at peace with their trial, yet inside they have turned off their connection to the *Unseen Power*. You are the only one who really knows what strength is inside you.

Often I find clients struggling with the notion of a religious obligation to forgive someone who has caused them harm. Many religions will teach that forgiving someone will bring you peace. But the strength to forgive someone who has harmed you may take years to achieve and may not be accomplished in this lifetime.

Skilled spiritual leaders can be very helpful during a difficult trial or trauma. However, I would encourage spiritual guides to tread delicately on the topic of forgiveness. Some people with a religious background might not know how to help you in your trials and might say statements such as: "This was God's will," or "God won't give you more than you can handle," or "Others have it much worse than you." If you happen to hear these types of statements, you might find peace or anger.

Some spiritual guides might try to force a victim to remove all their bad feelings about a perpetrator and demand they demonstrate or profess some form of forgiveness in order to "move on." I never tell a client that they need to forgive someone who has harmed them, unless they bring up the idea that doing so might free them from continued pain. Some have found that forgiving someone relieves the pain and internal poison and allows for growth and freedom. If you come to this point in your life on your own and in your own time, it could be monumental in your growth. However, the decision to forgive should never be forced on you.

If you are a victim of a perpetrator, it is up to you to decide when and if you ever forgive someone. In my opinion, no spiritual leader or perpetrator should ask or demand that you give anything else to those who harmed you. I encourage you to seek your *Unseen Power* on your own or with help and choose when and how you find peace with your past trial or trauma.

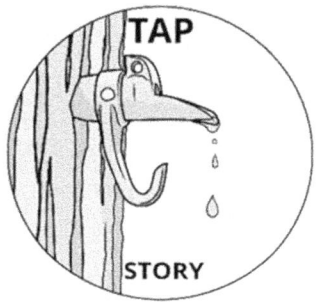

TAP Story: Loss of Husband to DUI driver - Ruth
Main TAP Tool: Unseen Power
Low Point/Stress Point: There has been an accident.

Trial Story: Many years ago, I worked in the prison facilitating family therapy with my friend and co-worker Ruth. We helped families prepare for the return of their addict family members being released from prison. During this time, Ruth's husband Brian was hit by a drunk driver. Both were injured. The other driver had a broken arm. Brian was conscious and told paramedics to take the other injured driver to the hospital first. However, his decision quickly turned fatal for him as he soon died from his injuries.

Growth Actions: The day eventually came when the drunk driver was sentenced for killing Brian. Ruth had decided to speak at the sentencing as a victim. To the surprise of many in the room, which included many of their twelve children, Ruth asked the judge for some leniency in the length of the sentence.

There was never any issue about forgiving the individual. She knew she had to forgive as a way of honoring her husband. Further, while she knew the perpetrator did not wake up thinking, "I'm going to drive impaired and take out someone on the road," the truth of the matter was that he did. Her husband died on their youngest daughter's birthday. Many of her children were not at the point in their personal growth where they could show leniency for the perpetrator and were actually upset with her.

TAP to Strong Growth: Years later, some still are. Some of them were also upset when Ruth testified at the parole hearing for this man five years later, requesting that he be granted parole. Again, this was a way of honoring her husband and based on the hard work the perpetrator accomplished while incarcerated. For her, real forgiveness was not accepting the behaviors that led to this incredible loss; it was striving to maintain honor, dignity, and then find peace for herself.

TAP to Lifetime of Growth: Ruth continued to work with addicts in prison and decided to go back to school to receive her PhD. She eventually became a university professor and often travels the world to help refugees and work with international social work students. She's a genuine example of someone who was able to turn her tragedy into a strength.

If you are the one in need of forgiveness from someone else, never ask your victim for forgiveness. You may apologize, pay restitution, privately hope for and even pray for your victim, but you should never ask them to forgive you in order to feel better about yourself. The best thing you can do is show by your observable actions you have changed your life.

Having said that, we all must forgive ourselves for past actions towards ourselves or others. I often see a client who has destroyed their family relationships or participated in degrading acts and feels stuck in an unreasonable, self-imposed hopelessness. When you have done all you can do to repair past actions, you may need to turn to an *Unseen Power* to help you move on with your life. Caring spiritual guides, more qualified than myself, should be able to help you with your journey.

You may or may not believe in an *Unseen Power* that can help you with your trial; this is your choice. The result of general research on helping others recognizes that many people do find their belief in an *Unseen Power* is helpful when they are confronted with very challenging trials or trauma.

My *Unseen Power* is God, and I feel He has guided me with the spirit to accomplish anything good in my life. I can't deny that He has guided or prompted me to work with specific people and has assisted with my career. I could never have overcome the trials in my life without His influence, and any successes in this life have been due to His guidance. In order to survive trials in life, I rely on family, friends, co-workers, therapists, books, religion, and my God.

The questions in this exercise will challenge you to realize that you may need to rely on a power greater than yourself to overcome trials. You control the power switch. You must decide when you're ready to use that power. You are the only one who can turn that switch on to request more power to be sent to you. You are the only one who can begin the process to seek and ask for help from those who specialize in these *Unseen Powers* and can guide you to the path of recovery.

Family, friends, and professionals can only do so much to help you overcome trials. Many of you will need to find that unseen or invisible power to achieve a healthy outcome.

Some call it an *Unseen Power* or Religion, some Nature, others Attitude or Hope. Imagine you are the plug and must decide if you will seek the invisible power.

1. Think of some instances in the past that an *Unseen Power* has helped you to overcome trials.

2. How has your view of your *Unseen Power* changed after your trial?

3. Who might help you draw on or find more power now?

4. What self-soothing techniques can you use to strengthen your internal power?

5. What will you DO to strengthen your internal power supply this week?

Internalization: Help Someone – Go and Teach Someone this Life Tap.

TRIAL TAPPERS

Record your thoughts...
_____
_____
_____

Record what you are grateful for...
_____
_____
_____

Record your commitment to positive action...
_____
_____
_____

Recap: Sometimes the only help can come from your *Unseen Power*. Some will grow towards this power, and some will pull away during trials. Forgiveness is not required for growth, but it may help.

As a Trial Tapper I draw on Unseen Power to help me overcome any trial.

• CHAPTER 6 •

TAP #5: Tap Your Supports during Unexpected Storms – Prepare for the Worst!

"Past unexpected trials in life have prepared you for the unexpected trials that will predictably be in your future."

TAP Overview: This TAP will help you prepare for future expected and unexpected storms and trials that may come. It will help you identify the trials you are prepared to face and the trials you hope will never come. Even I, an experienced therapist, need help from time to time.

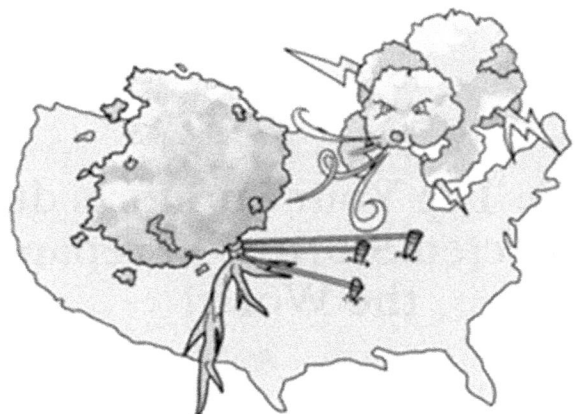

Tapping Supports during Unexpected Storms

This visual example is *Tap Your Supports during Unexpected Storms*. Imagine if you would, a background map representing the United States of America. In the middle is an oversized tree being blown over by a storm from the East Coast. The tree has very small roots on the east side and deep roots on the west side. There are three ropes tied to the tree and staked into the ground attempting to keep the tree from being blown over.

Preparing for unexpected storms is a visual lesson I have been using more and more over time. While I was doing my graduate work in the state of Colorado, a strange fall storm hit and blew over an entire forest of six million trees. Many speculated that the trees must have been weakened by some disease or insect.

I followed this story over the next month as researchers discovered that no insects or disease weakened these trees. They were blown over by a windstorm that blew across the state from east to west.

Why would a simple storm knock over millions of trees that had endured years of deep snows, severe drought, lightning strikes, and gusty winds? The explanation was that for years storms blew past Colorado as they travelled from the West Coast towards the East Coast. The storm that destroyed these trees was unusual because the wind traveled or spun off the backside of a massive low-pressure system from the *east* side of the state towards the *west* part of the state. Scientists discovered that the trees' roots had grown strong on the *west* side of the trees and yet were very weak on the *east* side of the trees.

This story of being blown over by unexpected storms is a perfect analogy for what we occasionally experience in life.

It's a common practice for therapists to help clients prepare for future trials that can be anticipated; for example, how to address issues with your spouse or how to prepare for the approaching death of a parent. Often the suggestion is to reach out to *Helpful Others* like a family member, a friend, or perhaps a sponsor, as these types of people are very helpful in preparing for future trials.

Most people prepare for the obvious trials or storms that they can predict, but not for the *Unexpected Storms*, because they did not believe these would happen. The following are examples of possible *Unexpected Storms* that afflict people.

- An addict returns home for the holidays anticipating support from the family. Unexpectedly, a younger sibling offers the addict drugs. This is an *Unexpected Storm*.
- An individual struggles in his/her marriage and confides with a best friend for several months. Eventually,

this individual finds out the best friend is having an affair with his/her spouse. This is an *Unexpected Storm*.
- An addict struggles with cravings and calls on the sponsor for support. Unfortunately, the sponsor has relapsed and offers the addict drugs. This is an *Unexpected Storm*.

The obvious upcoming storms in my life include preparing for the eventual death of my parents and possible cancers that are inherent in my family's genes. My father suffers from cancer that is currently in remission, yet he has already prepared his funeral arrangements and discussed his passing with his children. I am working with medical doctors to detect early signs of cancer in me.

The *Unexpected Storms* are too unpredictable to list. I don't want to obsess over the worst things that could ever happen in this world, but I do want those supports in place so I am prepared for any that may occur. If you don't prepare for the *Unexpected Storms*, there's a good chance you will be blown over when one arrives.

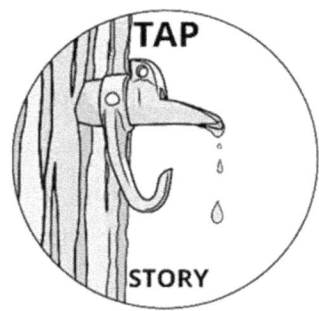

TAP Story: Brother's Suicide
Main TAP Tool: Unexpected Storms

Low Point/Stress Point: Cody has left a suicide video and we can't find him!

Trial Story: For years I have taught my clients that they need to prepare for the extreme worst scenarios in life. There I was, at age forty-nine, being put to the test when I received my own *Unexpected Storm*.

I am the oldest of four children born to my parents. After my parents divorced, my mother and her new husband decided to adopt my last two brothers. When Cody was adopted, I had already graduated from high school and was moving on to college. Because I was a new college student heavily involved in school, recently married and starting my own family, I only saw Cody on and off over the next few years. Our relationship was distant with there being twenty years difference in our ages.

During these years I was creating my own family, studying to become a social worker and working in a home for teenage girls who were demonstrating behavioral issues. Because of this, I could only watch from afar as my mother and her second husband began to have problems in their marriage. From time to time I would make attempts to encourage Cody, as I too had experienced my parents having marriage problems as a teen.

I was internally struggling with trying to assist with from afar with the stresses I began to see in Cody as his parents were overwhelmed with their marital issues.

I often found my advice fell short, as what parent wants to listen to the advice of their son or stepson? My mother's second marriage was facing what eventually became a divorce. My wife and I stepped in and offered to have both Cody and my youngest brother move into my home with my two boys. By now, Cody was about eleven years old, and I felt like I could finally have the positive "big brother" influence that we missed out on when he was younger. The next year was a good experience that my wife and kids will treasure forever. My boys, especially, had the opportunity to look up to Cody as their part-time big brother and cool uncle. I helped him with schooling, taught him how to pitch a baseball, and even disciplined him when needed.

Despite our efforts, Cody and his younger brother were returned to my mother and stepfather. That reunification did not last long. As my mother and her second husband ultimately divorced, Cody became a pawn in a nasty custody and visitation dispute that lasts beyond his death. Because Cody faced a tough teenage life, when he became an adult he eventually started doing things that took him away from his family. His lifestyle began to be radically different than mine as a law enforcement officer, and I began to see less and less of him over time. During the last few years before his death, he would only have contact with our mother. My brothers and sister could only get updates and send gifts to him through our mother, as he felt comfortable sharing with her his struggles with his own custody challenges with his two girls.

I had not seen Cody for a few years except on the Internet or in photos from my mother. The day he went missing, I did not even know where to begin to look for him. I was able to help my mother contact the police, and they were able to track his phone to a local mountain canyon.

Growth Actions: Being a law enforcement officer, the search team treated me as the coordinator between my mother and my former stepfather. To say that my relationship with my stepfather, Cody's adopted father, is strained is a huge understatement. We had not talked for years, yet I was able to put those angry feelings aside in order to assist in one single goal: to find Cody. When the search team finally found my brother and notified us of his death, both his parents were devastated. Despite their bitterness for each other, they mourned together at the loss of Cody. Hearing the news of Cody's death was very painful, and seeing these two parents fall apart was terrible to watch. Another brother of mine was with us at the notification and watched this horrific experience. Both of us hope to never have to endure the same pain with our children. Watching the pain of our mother and former stepfather moved us to mourn with them and even to pray with them as they requested.

TAP to Strong Growth: I share this story in full disclosure of our strained relationship near the end of his life. I have no desire to make attempts to rewrite history as some may foolishly do after someone has died. The truth hurts. From the moment we found Cody, my regret is only that he did not feel comfortable reaching out to me or any of his family or friends for help. His death was very difficult to accept, yet the support of family and friends was there to strengthen me in my time of need.

As I experienced the typical stages of grief that I will explain later in this book, it became clear to me that my relationship with Cody, although strained, was content. I am at peace with our relationship, as we had no ill words or arguments over the years, and I look forward to hugging him in the next life. The death of my brother was very traumatic for me and my family, but we are now looking towards the future for our own post-traumatic growth.

TAP to a Lifetime of Growth: The challenge of Cody taking his life had a profound impact on me, my family, and all his friends. Many have sought help with their own demons after seeing Cody fall victim to his. I dedicate this book to telling his story in an attempt to help others and will do so for the rest of my life.

Years ago an unexpected storm from the east blew over thousands of trees in a forest. Forest rangers discovered the trees had underdeveloped or weak roots on the east-facing side. Think of yourself as this tree. What *Unexpected Storms* are you preparing for in your future?

1. A tree's roots are its strength. What three strengths would others say you have?

2. What trials or storms have made you stronger?

3. Weather forecasters predict future storms. What storms or trials do you know are in your future?

4. What roots in your life are small and weak?

5. Post traumatic growth is always possible after a storm. Who will you ask for help to recover from a trial this week?

Internalization: Help Someone – Go and Teach Someone this Life TAP.

Record your thoughts...
_____
_____
_____

Record what you are grateful for...
_____
_____
_____

Record your commitment to positive action...

_____
_____
_____

Recap: Prepare for the future storms and trials in life that may come. What trials are you prepared to face? What trials do you hope will never come? Even as an experienced therapist with all these tools I need help from time to time.

As a Trial Tapper I prepare for the Unexpected Storms in my future.

SECTION III
RESILIENCE & EDUCATION

The following chapters will help you:
Recognize typical reactions to trials and traumas.
Gain a personal understanding of grief and negative cycles.
Know you are resilient and capable of overcoming all trials.
Identify unresolved trauma.
Understand that you should only put effort into things
you can control.

• CHAPTER 7 •

TAP #6: Tap Your Protective Vest – Balanced Life Helps!

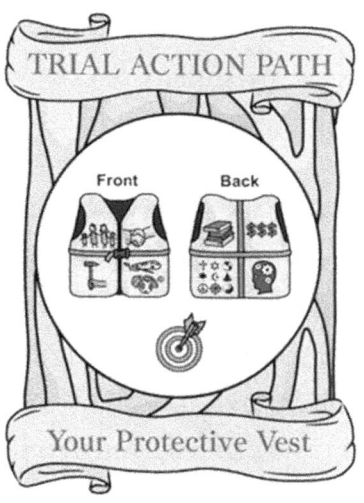

"Trials can affect all areas of your life, but a balanced life can protect you against all trials."

TAP Overview: This TAP describes how you should attempt to balance your life in order to protect yourself. Ignoring one aspect in your life can affect all others.

The next visual is *Tap Your Protective Vest*. This illustration shows the front and back of a life jacket or a bulletproof vest. Both are used to save your life. The front of the vest has four equal panels: a family, two hands shaking, a hand holding a hammer, sports equipment and an artist's paint board. These represent family, friends, field of work, and fun/fitness hobbies.

The back of the vest has four different panels: books; money; symbols representing different faiths, nature, meditation, and the earth; and a human head highlighting gears working in the brain. These four panels represent formal education, finances, faith, and mental fitness.

When teaching this particular lesson to inmates in prison, I would often walk into the classroom wearing a stab vest. When teaching students in the community, I would often walk in wearing my bulletproof vest. I also have a life vest or jacket that I use while I kayak. Any of these vests will help demonstrate the concept that we need to have balance in our life. The pictures on the vest are all the same size, denoting that a balanced life is needed for protection from trials.

These protective vests can help you survive a struggle or trial, but they won't keep you from getting hurt and even feeling pain. A bulletproof vest might stop a bullet, but you will often receive huge bruises and possibly broken ribs. A life vest may keep you afloat if you fall into the water from your kayak, but it won't stop you from getting bruised or cut on the rocks in the water.

Some law enforcement or military officers wear their bulletproof vest on the outside of their clothing, others wear it underneath their clothing, and some don't wear it at all. I always wear my vest underneath my clothing or concealed. Although wearing it up to twelve hours a day can be hot and uncomfortable, both my wife and I feel a little more protected facing the risks in this world.

I promised my wife years ago that I would always wear my vest in the community while at work. Even when the temperatures reach 100 degrees, I wear this vest out of love for my family. This story helps illustrate that there are two sides to the *Protective Vest* with its eight different areas that I need to pay attention to each day. There are obvious challenges in front of me, as well as those in the back of my mind or on my back. Even when some of these areas of my life are difficult, I need to put effort into each one out of love for myself, my family, and friends.

In the bottom of the illustration there is a red target with an arrow in it. Pinpoint which of these eight areas—Family, Friends, Field of Work, Fun/Fitness Hobbies, Formal Education, Finances, Faith, and Mental Fitness—are out of balance or nonexistent and make you vulnerable to attack.

When I teach this concept, I have my students draw pictures of vests of their own. Students have shown me their illustrations with entire panels removed or multiple red targets attacking different sections. Sometimes the Field of Work panel is very big, the Friends and Fun/Fitness Hobbies panels very small, and the Mental Fitness panel has a red vulnerable target on it. I tell my students that I would never go kayaking with missing panels on my life vest, nor wear my bulletproof vest missing entire sections. We must constantly pay equal attention to all panels or risk being defenseless when a big trial hits us.

Law enforcement or military officers are always looking to investigate potential problems and risks. To keep themselves and others safe, they must be aware of their position in relation to people around them. You also should always be on the lookout for potential problems or weak areas in your life. Be aware of your social position in relation to those around you, such as with your partner, children, friends, and the community. Knowing where you are vulnerable, such as in the areas of mental health or finances, will help you plan for addressing these areas.

Officers often have utility belts with multiple items such as a gun, pepper spray, flashlight, Taser, batons, and ammunition to help them deal with different situations and risks. They wear these around their waist for easy access when needed. A construction worker needs other tools. The utility bags around their waist consist of things like nails, hammer, measuring tape, pencils, etc.

Upon completion of this book, you will have a greater knowledge of what areas of your *Protective Vest* need attention, along with a full utility belt with different tools to use during trials in your life. You may not need all the tools/TAPs, nor use them all at the same time, but you will have them available to you for future use. Pay attention to every tool because your life may depend on them.

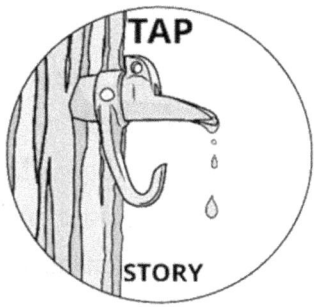

TAP Story: Family Man
Main TAP Tool: Protective Vest
Low Point/Stress Point: We might have lost a lot of money.
Trial Story: Jason Webb is a good example of someone who attempts to balance all eight areas of the *Protective Vest*.

1. Family: He and his wife Melanie have seven beautiful children.
2. Field of Work: He is the program director of a residential treatment program.
3. Friends: He has many friends.
4. Fun/Fitness Hobbies: He is an avid fisherman and takes his children fishing with him year-round. All of his children are involved in sports activities, and he often coaches their teams.
5. Formal Education: He has a master's degree in social work.
6. Faith: He is dedicated to his faith and has voluntarily served in many leadership positions in his church

7. Finances: He is raising his family in the only home he has ever purchased. He feels he has been making good investments toward retirement
8. Mental Fitness: As a clinical social worker, he has been keenly aware of his mental state and has been willing to seek advice from others when needed. He wrote a book called *The Reality of Perception.*

Despite having a balanced life, even Jason had a TAP to follow. Here is his story in his own words:

"The thing is, besides my daytime job, I got involved in buying real estate properties to rent out. I bought an apartment fourplex, which for the most part paid for itself. I had also invested some money which did well for a year. After a year my financial adviser asked if he could take my money from one investor and give it to another investor with the same rate of return. I trusted his advice and moved my investment. Unfortunately, I had unwisely borrowed money from a bank against my property because the return payments on my investment the first year were so good, and I invested it in this new opportunity. In reality, I soon found that I was swindled by the second man in an apparent Ponzi scheme, and I never saw a dime again. I lost all the money.

"Being a victim of this fraudster meant now I was in a position where I needed to pay the money back to the bank, and I didn't have the resources to do so. With the bills mounting and in a moment of despair, I once brought up possibly filing for bankruptcy to my wife. My wife did not take this well. She actually said to me, 'You signed your name on a piece of paper stating you would pay the money back. You will pay every dime back.' I agreed with my wife and knew we needed to find a way to pay back the bank. The problem was that the economy had just crashed, so we were unable to sell the fourplex and pay off the loan.

Growth Actions: "Then, as if by chance, something amazing happened. I am a therapist and had the idea to turn my fourplex into a sober-living home for addicts just coming out of rehab. By doing this, I could charge per person for those living in the facility and not just per the four units to generate more income.

"Instantly it became crystal clear to me how to apply for a city license and restructure my idle property that was barely covering expenses into a facility making more money than before.

"So, I started the long process of licensing my fourplex as a sober home with the city. But I didn't stop there. I held open houses with the neighbors to explain how I would be helping the community. I eventually gained the approval of both the city and the neighbors.

"Once I was given the license to move forward, I began advertising and filling up my facility with people in recovery. Besides providing a place to sleep, I also started giving these addicts therapy at night after I finished my work at my daytime job.

TAP to Strong Growth: "During this time my wife was able to stay home and take care of the children. She also helped manage our finances in a way that helped us cut back on expenses without sacrificing time with the family. Living on a limited budget was a family effort. We found sanity and peace through our faith in God. We continued to find time for me to coach my children's sporting events. We went on family campouts. We attended church together. After five years of this combined effort, we were able to sell the fourplex and pay back every dime we had lost in the bad investment.

TAP to a Lifetime of Growth: "We can honestly say our integrity and commitments have value. It felt good to own up to my word. I have become a lot smarter when it comes to investing. I have learned valuable lessons that will continue to guide my life. Most of all, I have found out that the secret to happiness is lining up my actions with my values."

Law enforcement officers feel safer when wearing a bulletproof vest. Your success overcoming traumas and trials in life depends on maintaining a careful balance between Family, Friends, Field of Work, Fun/Fitness Hobbies, Formal Education, Finances, Faith, and Mental Fitness.

1. How is your Family a protection to you during trials?

2. How can Friends help you during trials?

3. How can your Field of Work be productive during trials?

4. How can Fun/Fitness Hobbies be helpful during trials?

5. How can a Formal Education be helpful during trials?

6. How will living Financially Responsibly help you during trials?

7. How will focusing on your internal Faith be helpful during trials?

8. How will Mental Fitness help you during trials?

Internalization: Help Someone – Go and Teach Someone this Life Tap.

Record your thoughts...

_____
_____
_____

Record what you are grateful for...
_____
_____
_____

Record your commitment to positive action...
_____
_____
_____

Recap: You can make attempts to balance your life in order to protect yourself. Failing to focus on one aspect in life can affect all others.

As a Trial Tapper I identify those areas in my life that help protect me during trials.

• CHAPTER 8 •

TAP #7: Tap Your Yoyo Grief Cycle – Reality of Grief!

*"Grief is the reality of trials in life,
yet empowerment is the result of a life of grief."*

TAP Overview: This TAP will emphasize that recovery from grief can be achieved with practice. Patterns for recovery are predictable and can be understood. Once understood, your grief and the grief of others can be normalized.

The visual lesson that goes along with this TAP is how to *Tap Your Yoyo Grief Cycle*. Imagine the many different phases of a yoyo as it travels up and down. I've found that this visual of the cycle of grief is easy to understand because many people feel like painful memories continue to surface and resurface in their life. The imagery of the action of a yoyo can help us understand the steps of the grief cycle made famous by Kubler-Ross. I have made one modification to his cycle which I will explain below.

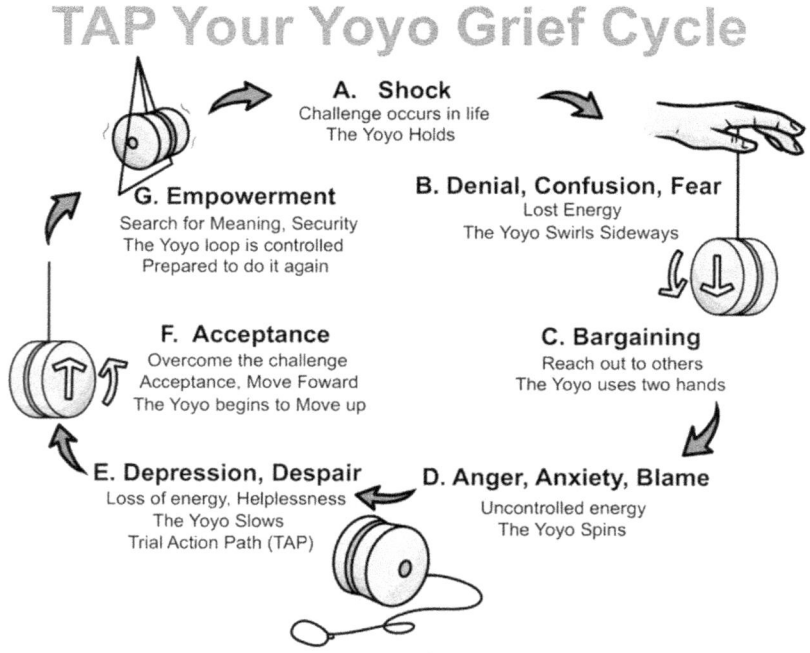

Successfully completing the grief cycle requires specific steps. Just as a yoyo moves down and then upward again in a predictable cycle, the grief cycle generally follows a predictable pattern too. Follow the steps of the grief cycle in the visual above, beginning at the top of the cycle (A. Shock) and progressing in a clockwise motion until you return again to the top. Let's walk through the grief cycle, stage by stage.

Stage A is the shock that occurs when the challenge first presents itself. If someone hands you a yoyo and says do some tricks, you might freeze. It takes time for you to comprehend what is happening when a major trial enters your life.

Stage B is the denial, confusion, or fear that occurs during the challenge. When you begin using a yoyo, you attach it to your finger and let the yoyo drop. This freefalling motion represents the confusion and fear that many feel during a major trial.

Stage C is the bargaining phase of your challenge, or when you reach out to others asking for help, unsure of how far you are going to plummet.

Stage D is the anger, anxiety, and blame you place on those who gave you this challenge in the first place. At this point our yoyo has reached the end of its rope, and it is spinning with uncontrolled energy.

Stage E is the despair or depression that occurs when you have no energy. You feel hopeless and believe that you are not capable of fixing the problem. Here the yoyo is stuck at the bottom of the cycle, motionless and unable to function. On the TAP Emotional Growth Chart, this stage coincides with the Weaken State just before you decide to make a positive change toward recovery.

Stage F is acceptance, such as when you begin to overcome the challenge by moving forward. Here the yoyo is working again and being pulled back up.

Stage G, the final stage, is a phase I've added to the Kubler-Ross Grief Cycle. I call it the Empowerment stage. This is where you find security, meaning, and growth as you have successfully endured both the initial shock and the TAP to Growth of depression. You are in this stage once you accept the reality of the trial and have grown to a point where you can control your actions. You are also empowered with new skills to survive future trials for a lifetime of growth.

Tapping your *Yoyo Grief Cycle* is simply understanding that after any major trial you will experience: A. Shock or Disbelief; B. Denial, Confusion, or Fear; C. Bargaining by reaching out to others; D. Anger, Anxiety, or Blame; E. Depression or Despair; F. Acceptance to begin moving forward; and G. Empowerment to endure this cycle again. These steps are normal reactions to abnormal events.

With practice, you can become skilled and perform technical tricks as you manipulate a yoyo. Your success in playing with the yoyo requires your energy as you move the toy repeatedly up and down. The key to understanding the grief cycle is to know that much like the yoyo going up and down, this cycle will be repeated multiple times in life. Recognizing the stages of this cycle will better prepare you for the cycles to come. Just know that grief after a trial and/or trauma is typical. However, you should not compare your experience and reactions with how others react to the same trial.

An example of the grief cycle in my life has been the months following my brother's suicide. I experienced each of the stages of this cycle drawn out over several months. I followed the typical path of Shock, Guilt, Depression, and then finally into the stage of Empowerment when I began writing this book on the six-month anniversary of my brother's death. I was required to experience this *Yoyo Grief Cycle* again three months later during the Christmas holiday. The difference this time was that I was able to go through every stage within a matter of days instead of months. I was better prepared to go through this *Yoyo Grief Cycle* again at the one-year anniversary of my brother's death.

When you or anyone you know experiences a large trauma or trial in life, a therapist will usually explain the stages of grief. When you're in the middle of the cycle, these different stages are often confusing or easily forgotten. I've found that using this image of playing with the yoyo is a simple way to explain the cycle. I emphasize that after you pass through the Despair stage, you will reach the stage of Empowerment which enables you to use new-found life skills.

Working a yoyo requires effort and energy to make it work. Pulling yourself back up out of the stage of Depression or Despair is often the hardest part of this cycle as explained in the TAP viewpoint. Sometimes just doing basic chores is challenging. In extreme cases I ask clients to begin with the basics: get out of bed, take a shower, or get dressed for the day. If you are currently reading this book and are having trouble with these basic tasks, seek help from others, which may include family, friends, a physician and/or therapist.

You can be in different stages of the grief cycle while dealing with different trials. For example, when entering the *Yoyo Grief Cycle* due to a possible loss of employment, you may also experience health problems or the death of a family member.

I have noticed a recurring event has been happening in my life since my brother's death. I have experienced several brief *Yoyo Grief Cycles* as I have been reminded of clients I've worked with who have taken their own lives or were killed.

The grief experienced from the death of a loved one is a universal experience. The Christian religion relates a story in the Bible when even Jesus experienced grief from the death of a friend, Lazarus. After arriving at the home of Lazarus' grieving sisters, Martha and Mary, seeing all the mourners, and seeing the family experiencing grief, the Bible relates: "Jesus wept" (John 11:35). Later when Jesus went to the grave to raise Lazarus from the dead, he demonstrated his grief once again. "Jesus therefore again groaning in himself cometh to the grave" (John 11:38). Grief is difficult for everyone!

When it comes to grief and processing the loss of a loved one, there are many ways to move forward. I typically don't like to go to viewings, but I will attend funerals. In the case of my brother's death, I assisted my mother with her own private viewing a few days before the funeral services. Family and friends organized a benefit concert and the release of lanterns over a lake. Some of my family members really enjoyed releasing the lanterns, and I found more connection by planting the flowers left from the reception around my house. I spent the next several months adding more plants to my yard, including four maple trees.

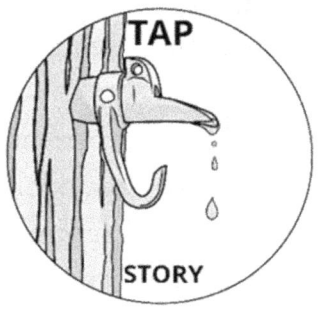

TAP Story: Death of a Daughter

Main TAP Tool: Yoyo Grief Cycle

Low Point/Stress Point: Why do I have to experience the death of another daughter?

Trial Story: I know a woman who lost her first daughter at birth. This happened more than sixty years ago. In those days the medical staff handled death differently. The baby was born deceased, and the nurses never even let this woman see her child before they took her away. How is this even possible? This seems so cruel now, and yet in those days they thought they were protecting her from pain. Not seeing the child was not the worst of it. Her husband was not informed as he was away at work for several months, and they didn't know where he was. The grandfather took it upon himself to arrange for the burial of the child while this mother was still in the hospital recovering. Neither parent got see their child before its burial, and both were only able to visit the grave. I can't even imagine the pain this woman had to endure of having the child grow inside her, but never being able to see it, and then having to endure the loss alone until her husband was located. The death of her daughter was very trying on her as a young mother, and she needed the support of family and friends to go through the *Yoyo Grief Cycle*.

Growth Actions: This woman experienced extreme loss and sorrow, and yet she decided to try again for another child.

TAP to Strong Growth: As she continued with her life, she eventually had five more children, and she has remained close to them her entire life. Like anyone who has lost a child, she briefly experiences *Yoyo Grief* every year around the holidays and anniversaries of her first child's birth/death. Experiencing the grief of losing a child is more than most parents should have to do. In another painful trial, she experienced another tragic loss at the age of seventy-nine when her oldest daughter succumbed to cancer. The pain of losing two children is a trial I hope never to face. She mourns the loss of her children, yet her religion and faith are what keeps her going.

TAP to a Lifetime of Growth: This woman's passion has always been her children, her grandchildren, and now her great-grandchildren. She makes a point of always letting her family know how much she loves them and that she would do anything in the world to help them. She continues to experience worry about her loss from time to time, yet now she can share with others what she has learned from both trials.

Passing through grief is different for many people, yet most will experience a very similar cycle.

TRIAL TAPPERS

Many historians believe yoyos were first invented in China around 1000 B.C., and humans have been experiencing the grief cycle for even longer. In 1969, after studying the common grief stages, Kubler-Ross outlined a grief cycle that professionals have been teaching ever since. I use the imagery of a yoyo in order to help you remember this natural process. I modified the cycle, adding a stage called Empowerment, because the experience that you gain when you rise up from grief is powerful.

Stages of the *Yoyo Grief Cycle*:
- Shock/Loss - Yoyo holds
- Denial - Yoyo begins to fall
- Bargaining, Reach out to others - Yoyo needs two hands
- Anger, Anxiety, Blame - Yoyo spins
- Depression, Despair – Yoyo slows and might stop
- Acceptance - Yoyo begins to move up
- Empowerment – Yoyo loop is controlled. Prepare to repeat.

Completing this cycle makes you stronger and prepares you for future trials.

1. When have you completed the *Yoyo Grief Cycle* in the past?

2. What does completion look like to others?

3. What does it look like to others if you stop moving forward?

4. What might be keeping you from moving forward?

5. If you are stuck on a step, who can help you move ahead?

6. Who or what helped you complete this cycle in the past?

7. All yoyo spins are different. Some people will skip stages or change the order. Where are you on the loop?

8. Where can you move the negative energy into something positive?

9. How can you plan for the next cycle to begin?

Internalization: Help Someone – Go and Teach Someone this Life Tap.

Record your thoughts...
_____
_____
_____

Record what you are grateful for...
_____
_____
_____

Record your commitment to positive action...
_____
_____
_____

Recap: Recovery from grief can be achieved with practice. Patterns for recovery are predictable and can be understood. Once understood, your grief and the grief of others can be normalized.

As a Trial Tapper I believe no matter how painful the trial I can accept a new reality and recover.

• CHAPTER 9 •

TAP #8: Tap Your Pit of Despair – Start Climbing, Get Out!

*"Pits of despair may accompany your trials,
yet belief in oneself will repair the despair"*

TAP Overview: Sometimes in life we all feel stuck in a pit of despair. This TAP will help you understand that climbing out of pits may take time and effort. It will give you suggestions to help you avoid falling in the same pits in the future. It will help you recognize that setbacks in life are normal and growth is possible once you are out of the pit.

The visual illustration is how to *Tap Your Pit of Despair*. The picture shows a dark pit or cave with a ladder at the bottom leading up to a sunlit opening above.

Sometimes in life you may experience a trial that leads you to the bottom of the *Yoyo Grief Cycle*, or a *Pit of Despair*. You might feel lost and hopeless, struggling to find a way out. Ending up in this pit might have started from circumstances out of your control, from your own actions, or from the actions of others. No matter how you ended up in this position, you need to begin making efforts to climb out of the pit. You may need to call out for help from people who haven't fallen into the pit.

When working with clients, I find that many of them relate to this image. Some common pits they are working to climb out of include addictions, abusive relationships, mental health challenges, legal problems, chronic illnesses, and financial struggles.

Admitting or acknowledging that the place you are in is uncomfortable and unproductive is the first step toward progress. Once you are able to identify which pit you might be experiencing, you can set goals about climbing out. A key to successfully climbing out of a pit is to identify what targeted behaviors you can control as you begin moving forward.

I have worked with clients who recognized they needed help getting out of the pit by setting some achievable goals with them. Many expressed positive thoughts as they began their journey. They would do well for a while and then fall back into the pit around six and sometimes twelve months into the journey. This pattern became so predictable that I often tell the following story as a warning.

Almost everyone has experience climbing a ladder. I have a very tall ladder which allows me to reach the gutters on the second story of my house. One day I was high on my ladder, and in a moment of distraction I missed a step. I slid down a few rungs before I caught myself. Obviously, this scared me, and I became especially focused for the remainder of my work on the ladder. After telling this story to a client, I explain my observations about the six-month and twelve-month pitfalls and then explain that while I may have slid down a few rungs on the ladder, I chose to pay attention and to continue climbing instead of letting go and falling to the ground. I never forget that climbing experience; I remember it each time I climb any ladder. Can you visualize what happened to me and how you might feel if it happened to you?

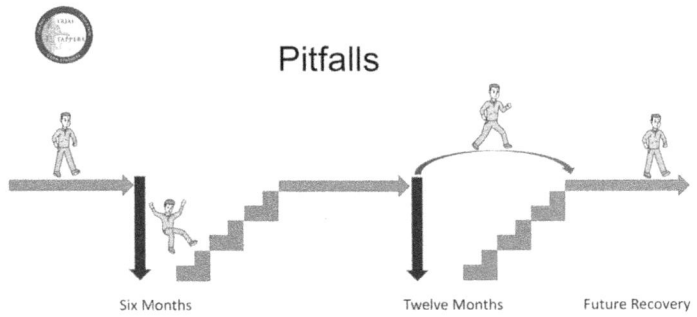

There are many reasons for people to fall into these pitfalls at six months and twelve months. For someone dealing with addiction, things often go well until they run into an old friend or stop going to counseling or support groups. Someone struggling with the loss of a family member will often say that an anniversary of the death causes them to relive the *Yoyo Grief Cycle*. Someone with mental health issues will often tell me they were feeling so good that they decided to stop seeing their doctor and taking their medications. Often, they see it as a reward for doing so well. But they return to old thoughts or behaviors that lead them to fall back into the pit.

Occasionally, the TAP Emotional Growth Chart and the TAP to Strong Growth come into play. They may have been using some of the previous taps to move forward. They've identified their need for growth, they have begun to balance their lives with the *Protective Vest*, they elicit the help of others, they begin to have some higher goals and start demonstrating some positive behaviors. Then around the six-month or twelve-month mark, they get hit with another major trial and fall back into a pit or return to the bottom of the *Yoyo Grief Cycle*. Sometimes this is self-induced; other times it's the result of needing more practice with their new skills.

Setbacks in life are normal. Everyone makes mistakes, but the key to being successful in making corrections is identifying what you did well and where you got off the path. With the assistance of *Helpful Others*, climbing out of the pit towards recovery should become easier, based on successful climbs in the past. If you can't move on after a trial, you might need professional help to get out of your *Pit of Despair*.

TRIAL TAPPERS

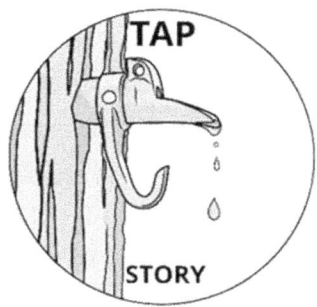

TAP Story: Depression

Main TAP Tool: Pit of Despair

Low Point/Stress Point: I'm at work and so depressed that I crawled under my desk.

Trial Story: My friend Brad Anderson has written a book called *The View From Under My Desk*, which is about his life-long struggle with depression. He has been very successful training many people from major corporations, yet he's always struggled with depression.

Growth Actions: Despite his challenges with depression, Brad kept showing up for work every day until he retired a few years ago. He has helped write books for his employers and even authored one himself. He makes efforts to spend time with his family and has developed a support group to help himself.

TAP to Strong Growth: Brad has sought professional assistance from many doctors and therapists. He attempted every treatment that psychiatry and therapy had to offer, but he received no benefits from these efforts. He is known as a depressive who is treatment resistant, yet he continues to study emerging treatment methods that show promise. Despite his positive actions, Brad has recognized he will most likely never find a treatment that works for him, that he won't ever fully overcome his challenges with depression, and that he may struggle for the rest of his life. Acknowledging this, Brad decided to do his best and to write a book about his struggles. Admitting to himself that he struggled was important, but publishing it for the world to see was another challenge entirely.

TAP to a Lifetime of Growth: Why does Brad have to struggle with this illness? How will he benefit from telling his story to the world? Brad's mission is to help others recognize that many people struggle with depression from time to time. Sometimes it's situational and sometimes it's biological. Brad takes pride in professionally teaching companies about being emotionally healthy. He has a mission to help coworkers recognize the signs of depression in others in order to help support them during their time of trial. If you struggle with depression or know of someone who does, you might want to get a copy of his book.

Sometimes you will get stuck in a dark *Pit of Despair*. This could feel like loneliness, depression, addiction, hopelessness, or feelings of being lost. Imagine you are at the bottom of this pit looking up at the sunlight at the top of the ladder.

1. What trial in life has you trapped in a *Pit of Despair*?

2. List five "Core Beliefs" you have about why you think you belong trapped in this pit.

3. What will motivate you to take hold of the ladder and start climbing out?

4. When you slip down a rung of the ladder, what will you do to recover?

5. Who will you ask to help get out of your pit?

Internalization: Help Someone – Go and Teach Someone this Life Tap.

Record your thoughts...
_____
_____
_____

Record what you are grateful for...
_____
_____
_____

Record your commitment to positive action...
_____
_____
_____

Recap: Sometimes in life we all feel stuck in a *Pit of Despair*. Climbing out of pits may take time and effort. Avoid falling in the same pits in the future, but remember that setbacks in life are normal and growth is possible once out of the pit.

As a Trial Tapper I recognize past attempts at growth as positive.

• CHAPTER 10 •

TAP #9: Tap Your Trauma Trash Can – Empty the Hidden Trauma!

*"Silencing your trauma will lead to much strife,
but addressing your trauma will lead to a long life."*

TAP Overview: Hidden trauma will always resurface at some time in the future. Garbage cans not taken out will always stink. This TAP is intended to help you understand that your visible symptoms might be a result of past trauma. It will encourage you to avoid masking those internal reactions.

The visual lesson is *Tap Your Trauma Trash Can*. The image is of an old metal trash can that is full of so much trash that it's overflowing and falling onto the ground. Some of the debris includes an empty beer bottle, a milk carton, and scraps of food. The debris is labeled Anger, Depression, and Addictions. Above the trash can is a large military-type boot that is moving towards the top of the trash can. The boot is labeled Silence. The trash can is labeled with the words Trauma, Loss, and Abuse.

My job as a probation officer requires me to make unannounced home visits to both rich and poor homes which have something in common: Trash. They all have trash that needs to be taken out. Some homes only have a minor amount of garbage, and other homes have an extreme amount.

All of the previous TAPs have been preparing you for this most important concept of trauma. How do you deal with the extreme trials or traumas in your life? Someone once told me that not dealing with trauma is similar to not taking out the garbage. I have taken that example to heart as I help my clients relate to this image.

Think of your own home and the trash that needs be taken out. In my home we attempt to push the trash down further in the can until we're forced to take it out. The practice of repeatedly pushing down the trash inevitably leads to leaks, smells, and often spilt garbage on the floor. When I come across homes that refuse to take out the trash, the smell is sometimes overwhelming. Some people actually take the trash bags out of the can, yet leave the full bag next to that same can. Not only is the trash overflowing, but they are saving it!

Imagine that we all have a symbolic *Trash Can* inside our bodies. This can fills up with our emotions and feelings when we experience a trauma. As I mentioned at the beginning of this book, research shows that many of us have or will experience some form of trauma in our lifetime. Refusing to admit that we have these feelings and emotions after a difficult trauma will lead to this emotional garbage leaking, smelling, and dumping out unexpectedly.

Often the symptoms or reactions I see with my clients are their bits of garbage overflowing their emotional *Trash Can*. The leakage and smells might be anger, depression, or addiction. When the clients only want to address the symptoms and refuse to empty the emotional garbage can, they will predictably slow their growth and struggle with smaller trials in the future.

When I take my actual garbage out of my home, I take it to the street and give it to a professional who knows how to sort through it for recycling and turn it into new products for others to use.

I chose to empty my emotional garbage in relation to the suicide of my brother and the sexual abuse I experienced as a child. Family and friends were sympathetic to my pain, but it wasn't until I reached out to professionals that I was able to fully empty my emotional *Trash Can*.

I can tell you this truth from decades of experience: Getting past the observable symptoms to the underlying root of the problem is always the hardest part of the therapy. Often, people come to treatment with the initial symptom or surface or "safe" problem. Examples of obvious symptoms might be the following: addiction, marital problems, depression, anxiety, or anger.

For example, in working with men who have committed domestic violence towards their spouse, I would often find that the man was abused in some way during his early life. Although unresolved trauma does not excuse his behavior, it might be the root cause of his anger. Failing to talk about those feelings when the subject gets too close to the actual root of shame, anger, and trauma may encourage the man to act out violently instead of productively.

I once spent a year as a member of a university Institutional Review Board often called an IRB. My job was to review studies which researchers wanted to do on vulnerable incarcerated populations. After reviewing the proposals from the researchers, I would present my concerns to the entire board and make recommendations for changes to the study.

One researcher wanted to take service animal dogs into the prison to comfort prisoners during therapy sessions. Service animals are commonly used in therapy now. Like I mentioned in *Helpful Others*, my dog Charlie helps me when I come home from a long day. Many researchers now understand the impact animals can have to improve mood. My experience in the prison taught me that, in most cases, German Shepherds are the preferred breed of dog used to intimidate and restrain criminals. I eventually recommended approval for the study with the restriction of not allowing German Shepherds in the facility because of possible trauma the inmates may have experienced when being chased or restrained by law enforcement officers during a past arrest. Inmates participating in this study were already in prison and did not need to be re-traumatized by the sight or bark of this breed of dog.

Grief and sorrow after past trials will not impact you at the same level as the initial trauma. The effects or reactions of trauma on a person can be suppressed for years without anyone being able to identify the original source. Many who have experienced traumatic events show very little emotion during the actual experience. For example, victims of rape are known to freeze up or not exhibit any outward reactions about what happened; they're in shock. When some experience this type of extreme trauma their outward appearance may be stoic, but their internal emotions are extreme. When my abuser showed up at my brother's funeral, I re-experienced the trauma and froze momentarily. I did not say anything to anyone until later that night with my wife.

Failing to address these types of internal emotions will not prevent your body from feeling them. It will slowly react over the years as your brain continually reminds your body of the past. Your internal systems will start reacting. For example, as you read this chapter on trauma, in your head you might be saying things like, "I don't know if I want to continue reading." Also you might be experiencing some internal anxiety; your stomach might be aching; your foot might be lightly tapping; you might be sweating, becoming anxious, or feeling nervous; your heart might be racing or your head aching. You might be sitting perfectly still, but if I hooked you up to an electrocardiogram (EKG) heart monitor, I might see your heart rate or blood pressure increasing.

Addressing your trauma might be a deep subject that's difficult for you to talk about. Physical symptoms or complaints may be your body's typical reaction to unresolved, leaking garbage that needs to be addressed and possibly worked through. If you are having these types of thoughts or reactions, you might need the help of a professional counselor.

Once I can convince a client to address past traumas, their emotional release will sometimes be explosive. When you experience abusing substances, anxiety, anger, depression, self-harm, recurring memories or flashbacks that are unexpectedly triggered by experiences, sounds, or smells, your body might be communicating to you the need for professional assistance. If you are missing these warning signs, pay attention to helpful feedback from your family and friends.

WARNING! When you decide to address past trauma and take the steps for positive change, you will experience the TAP to Growth addressed at the beginning of this book. You will experience temporary stress and possibly flashbacks as you work through the trauma with a professional. However, I can tell you from experience that it will get better as you continue the process and grow stronger.

Failing to deal with and not empty your own emotional trash from past traumas will prevent you from successfully helping others going through a similar experience in the future. I have witnessed people attempt to help others with a particular trauma because they experienced something similar in the past. But often these helpful people fail to realize that they never truly emptied their own emotional *Trash Can*. Their past traumas leak out and contaminate those they are attempting to help.

The challenge will always be to admit and/or identify the root of the problem. The next step is to identify your core beliefs about the problem, accepting that you can't control the actions of others. Once you identify the actions you can control, you can make a plan to address the root of the problem and finding alternative paths to achieve the goal when you encounter obstacles.

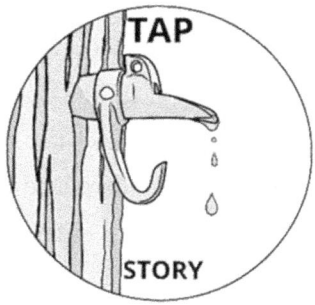

TAP Story: Sexual Abuse
Main TAP Tool: Trauma Trash Can
Low Point/Stress Point: Face to face with evil.
Trial Story: For years I have taught my clients that they need to address any unresolved traumas in their past. There I was at age forty-nine, being put to the test when I received my own *Unexpected Storm* that dug up my past trauma.

During my brother's funeral the most unbelievable thing happened to me. I was in the line greeting my brother's friends who came to pay their last respects when I was unexpectedly blindsided in the worst way. I suddenly found myself shaking the hand of the man who sexually abused me thirty-eight years earlier when I was eleven years old.

There I was, asking myself questions like: What is happening? Am I dreaming? Why can't I speak? Why can't I breathe? This had nothing to do with the fact that I was trying to endure the grief of attending my deceased brother's viewing just minutes before his funeral service. I was standing feet away from my deceased brother, emotionally drained from all that had happened over the past week. I kept telling myself I could make it through just a few more hours, but now I'm paralyzed.

I was confused, in shock, and couldn't move. A flood of memories and fear from my childhood made me freeze up. Another brother standing next to me noticed something was wrong because of my pale, blank stare and stepped between me and my perpetrator. Then I somehow managed to walk out of the church.

I was a victim of sexual abuse from age eleven to twelve by a boy four years older than myself. Without going into a lot of detail, I will just say that it was very traumatic. I had no experience with anything sexual. My parents had decided to let me stay at the home of a family friend so their fifteen-year-old son could help me memorize scripture needed to advance from the children's program in my church. I needed to memorize basic articles of faith in order to be ordained a deacon. Once all the adults left, the lessons being taught went from religion to sex, and the emotional, physical, and sexual abuse lasted for several hours. Eventually, my parents returned; however, I was in a state of fear that if I told anyone, my parents and siblings would be hurt. I wish I could say that this was the only time the abuse happened. A few weeks later, my parents left me alone with this teenager again and the sexual abuse continued. Some of the details are very vivid, and others I have chosen to block out. For the next few years I lived in fear every time our families made attempts to get together.

I was intimidated with actual threats of violence towards myself and my siblings, so I suffered this trauma in silence. Because my parents were dealing with their own trials during the end of their marriage, they did not see the behavior change in me. My parents' divorce actually stopped the abuse, as their friendship with my abuser's parents ended.

I grew up when Acquired Immunodeficiency Syndrome (AIDS) had just been discovered, and so I feared that I had been infected. This fear continued until I was tested when I turned nineteen. As a Christian I had had no other sexual relationships and chose to share my abuse with my fiancée prior to our marriage. We grew closer together due to my sharing the experience with her. For the next thirty-eight years, I felt I had moved on with my life, and I tried to forget the past abuse.

I had hoped to never meet my abuser face-to-face again. I never expected him to show up at my brother's funeral, let alone try to shake my hand and comfort me in my grief. My sorrow quickly turned to anger as I composed myself and returned inside to assist with the remaining proceedings of the funeral. Thankfully, there were so many people that I did not see my abuser for the remainder of the services. I hope he realized how inappropriate it was for him to show up to talk to me after all these years.

Growth Actions: I struggled in silence with this secret for many years. At age twenty-one, I decided to discuss these experiences with religious leaders. At age twenty-five, I informed my wife and mother of what had happened fourteen years prior. I asked my mother to inform my abuser and his parents that they were not welcomed at my wedding. Everyone was helpful and reassured me that I had done nothing wrong fourteen years earlier.

TAP to Strong Growth: The big problem was that I knew I needed to address any past traumas in order to help others. As I trained to become a therapist, I decided to put the therapy to the test and work through this trauma once again. It was, "Physician heal thyself first." It turns out that I did not truly resolve this trauma, and I recognize now that I might not have been ready to at that time. I only worked on symptoms and wasn't yet ready to open that old wound of abuse. Now as I look back, I realize I never really explored my feelings or reactions associated with the abuse. I might have talked about the events, yet I failed to admit the fears and embarrassment I had inside me about the abuse. I wanted it to all just go away so I would never have to deal with it again.

My plan to test myself occurred during my master's degree practical training. I chose the hardest field I could find—working with both victims and perpetrators of sexual abuse. I had reviewed assessments and treatment plans for these groups for more than twenty years, and I felt comfortable knowing I was helping other victims receive the treatment they need.

I had prepared myself for years on how to handle my own abuse situation. When those times of reliving the pain of my childhood came up, I could turn to family, friends, and my faith to help me. I thought I could face many challenges in life yet was not prepared for what happened at my brother's funeral.

After that I had to make some tough decisions. I have been a private and somewhat shy person all my life. The story of my sexual abuse has been a closely held secret few knew; I had not even shared my trauma with my children. If I was going to get real with myself and lead by example, then I would have to be open and honest with everyone.

In my professional life I hate being the center of attention. I prefer to work behind the scenes and not call attention to myself. Despite my reluctance to lead out, I felt the need to step out of the darkness and into the light if I wanted others to do the same. The thought of doing this scared me to death, and I had an internal debate with myself about why I couldn't just share my story about my brother's suicide and hide the sexual abuse? I told myself it would be embarrassing to let my friends, neighbors, family, and children know what happened. I have always struggled with people on social media who only share their accomplishments, thereby portraying their lives as "perfect." The natural desire for many people is to only talk about their successes in life and to skip past their setbacks or even failures. After a long internal struggle, I came to the realization that sharing my story of sexual abuse now is my declaration of freedom. The perpetrator threatened me as a child to make sure I remained silent, and for the most part I have done so for thirty-eight years. Now I choose to free myself from that shame, and I hope others will do the same.

Although I was strong enough to endure this *Unexpected Storm*, at age fifty I still turned to a therapist to undergo EMDR Therapy for several months in order to separate the newly colliding traumatic events of my brother's suicide and the past abuse once and for all.

While in therapy, it became clear to me that I needed to tell my story. I could have continued to hide my abuse from family, friends, clients, and the world. Shame and fear are the tools the abuser used to keep me quiet as a child and most of my adult life. The fact that he showed up to see me again after all these years caused me a lot of emotional pain. With the help of my wife and therapist, I decided to investigate him with the help of local police and to finally tell my story and file a police report. The statute of limitations might have run out on the abuse, but if the abuser has any other victims, my report will be on file in the town where he lives. I may not be able to prosecute him for the abuse, but I might be able to help another victim.

What I have learned is that I can share my personal experiences with you in this book, and my story will not be complete without telling you my biggest trauma and trial because I want you to do the same. I share this story not only to help me grow from my trial, but hopefully to help you address yours and grow. If my sharing of this trauma helps just one person, then it is worth it.

TAP to a Lifetime of Growth: My life's experiences helped prepare me for my current position in the community. My career has led me to attempt to protect other children from becoming victims of sex offenders. For many years I have been responsible for confirming the registration of all federal sex offenders in my state, which requires me to meet with each perpetrator individually. I have had many other opportunities to make an impact. Under the direction of the chief federal judge in the State of Utah, I have explained the electronic monitoring that we use with sex offenders to a delegation of foreign diplomats. I currently oversee the treatment and polygraphs of all federal sex offenders in my state.

We all experience trauma and trials during our lives. When we do not deal with our trauma, we stuff it into our emotional *Trash Can*. The more traumas we stomp down with silence, the more rot is created inside of us. With the passing of time, the *Trash Can* will start to stink and leak out at unexpected times.

1. Who in your life unconditionally supports you?

2. List three professionals you can always call on for help.

3. How do you define trauma?

4. What is a trauma you have seen someone else overcome?

5. What disturbing thoughts or smells do you try to avoid?

6. List something you have survived that you're comfortable sharing.

7. When have you unexpectedly dumped your trauma trash?

8. What did the mess look like to others?

9. Be strong. Identify any trauma you have not taken out or told to *Helpful Others*.

10. How has your silence turned to a smell or internal rot?

11. What do you risk by continuing to stomp down your emotions?

12. List three positive reasons to empty your trauma trash.

13. Show your post-traumatic growth by sharing your trial with someone you trust this week. Who will it be?

14. How might cleaning out this trauma trash change your life for the better?

Internalization: Help Someone – Go and Teach Someone this Life Tap.

Record your thoughts...

_____
_____
_____

Record what you are grateful for...

_____
_____
_____

Record your commitment to positive action...

_____
_____
_____

Recap: Hidden trauma will always resurface some day in the future. Garbage cans not taken out will always stink. Your symptoms on the surface might be a result of past trauma. Avoid masking the symptoms and reactions with abusive behaviors.

As a Trial Tapper I believe no matter how painful the trauma I can survive and thrive in the future.

SECTION IV
STRENGTHS & EMPOWERMENT

The final chapters will help you:
Free yourself from past trauma/trials.
Turn your pain into motivation that can help others.

TRIAL TAPPERS

• CHAPTER 11 •

TAP #10: Tap Your Outside Resistance – Get Motivated!

"Trials will come to every tree in the forest, yet adapting to trials will give you more force."

TAP Overview: Not everyone wants to see you succeed. Some will even attempt to knock you down. With time most trials will pass, and negative people in life will move on. This TAP will show you how to prove negative people wrong and overcome your trial.

This visual example is called *Tap Your Resistance*. The illustration is of a lonely maple tree encircled by a gopher, a termite, a hornet's nest, a snake, a woodpecker, and fungus on a tree.

The tree does not get to decide where it is planted or what type of sunlight or water it receives. It must rely on its roots to dig down deep into the soil to survive. This tree appears to be under attack by animals and disease. I use this visual with clients to help them understand the concept that sometimes in life, even though you're minding your own business, there are people that are going to cause you stress, discomfort, or harm.

Although your intentions are good, there are people in this world who momentarily cross your path and cause you stress and discomfort. Some may be trying to keep you down. Others may challenge you to do something that might help you to grow in the future.

At one of my previous places of employment, I had a supervisor who was misguided as to how he could use funds from my department for another department. I questioned his actions in person and sent several emails to him and others in my department. Those continual reminders fostered a contentious relationship between us.

After several years the work environment became hostile and intimidating, including ridicule and profanity. Because this happened early in my working career, I did not know that I had options and could challenge his outbursts and profanity towards me, and so I began looking for new employment. I felt like a young kid once again being bullied by someone more powerful. I hated talking to my boss, and the interactions we had were more and more confrontational.

Prior to my leaving, outside auditors found the misappropriated funds that I had warned about for years. My supervisor attempted to blame me for the errors and placed my decisions under investigation. I could not believe I was being blamed for the actions of my boss. I reluctantly endured the accusations and investigation. I made it clear that I had known my supervisor was misguided and had challenged his decisions for years. After enduring the investigation, I was exonerated from any wrongdoing when I produced all the letters and emails I had sent and saved over the years.

This was a valuable experience that taught me that though negative people will come into my life from time to time, they will eventually move on and that I will have to stand up for my rights. Enduring the investigation was difficult, but it was easy compared to the following weeks, in which I had to endure my supervisor confronting and yelling at me every chance he had. Eventually he was demoted and moved from my department.

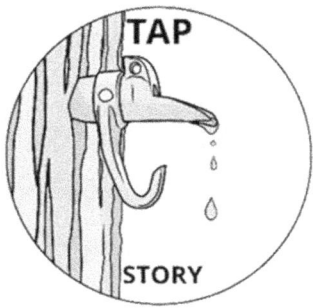

TAP Story: Academy

Main TAP Tool: Resistance

Low Point/Stress Point: I could lose my job. What am I going to tell my family and friends?

Trial Story: When I was hired to become a federal probation officer, I needed to attend the Federal Law Enforcement Training Center, often called FLETC, in South Carolina. In order to graduate from the academy, I was required to earn a passing score when shooting a pistol.

Growth Actions: I know it is ironic being a social worker required to carry a gun, but this is a job requirement. When I arrived at the academy, I was already proficient in shooting my gun, had passed the required shooting course many times, and felt well prepared to pass this requirement again. When I was hired my local firearms instructor issued me a gun that was previously owned by a former officer, and I took this gun with me to the academy.

I began to have a big trial I could not believe was happening. Shortly after my training began, I started having issues with my gun. Occasionally, I would have problems firing all the required bullets in the time allotted. I would pull the trigger, and one out of ten times it would not fire. Some days it would work fine, and others it would not.

TAP to Strong Growth: The crazy thing was that because I failed to fire all my bullets in the allotted time, my practice scores continued to drop. Instead of getting better, I got worse. When I told the range masters my gun was not working, he didn't believe me, and at least one instructor belittled me by stating the issue was "in my head, not the gun." To my dismay, the few times the instructor fired my gun, it fired normally, which seemed to confirm his accusations.

My decreasing scores brought more unwanted attention from instructors, and I felt humiliated in front of my peers. The possibility of my failing to graduate and possibly losing my career became a constant concern. I worried about what I would tell my family and friends if I lost this job. How would I provide for my family? I was feeling a lot of stress, and yet my wife was encouraging as we talked each night on the phone. I tried to use positive thoughts to overcome my challenge and keep telling myself I could overcome this, but positive thinking was not helping my scores. And at the end of each day, I was required to return to the firing range to take remedial lessons and put in extra practice.

TAP to a Lifetime of Growth: In order to survive the belittling looks from others, I had to hyper focus on controlling my inner thoughts and emotions when I went to the range each day. I knew I could pass the course, as I had done so many times prior to arriving at the academy. I had to practice calming myself despite being heckled by my instructor and my gun not functioning.

The last week of training arrived, and we began practicing for the final qualifications. My gun was acting up so much that I literally had to use two fingers to pull the trigger. Even then it did not always work. After another failed test, I challenged my instructor to try and pass the test himself using my gun. He accepted the challenge, and as I expected, but much to his surprise, the gun did not work! I can't even explain how relieved I felt.

Instantly he turned my gun over to the head range master who discovered that, not only was my trigger broken, but it was the wrong type and was not used by anyone in the entire federal law enforcement system. I had been issued a used gun with an outdated "New York" trigger that should have been replaced years prior. After they fixed my gun, I returned to the range and passed with a qualifying score.

I finally felt like I was not the failure the past weeks had shown. The entire time I was training with my academy peers, I had some of the worst scores in practice, and my confidence in my abilities struggled at times. Once my gun was fixed, I had no problem qualifying and passing my final test. After everyone had achieved the qualifying scores, we participated in a head-to-head shooting tournament to determine the best shooter in our group. Later that day all the academy graduates and the instructors got together at a local restaurant to celebrate our graduation and accomplishments. Much to the instructors' surprise, I had won the tournament and was given the title of "Top Gun."

I tell this story to illustrate that life can hit you with some odd and unexpected challenges. I never expected to be labeled a poor student after completing my graduate degree. I never expected to have trouble with a skill I had previously mastered. I never expected to be singled out as a poor performer, because I consider myself to be somewhat competitive. I did learn to be more resilient despite what others were saying to, and about, me. I knew I was better than what my scores reflected, and it took patience and effort to prove I could overcome the challenge.

I challenge you to use the trials people place before you to motivate you to continue to grow stronger.

The reality of resistance in this visual story is that the tree will often outlive most challenges that it currently faces, and you will outlast those negative people around you.

Some trials quickly pass, but others take more time to recover from. Every tree in the forest will experience hardships in one form or another. Imagine yourself as this tree facing trials. You can learn to adapt and grow stronger as you face these problems one at a time.

1. What is a medium trial you have overcome?

2. What trial do you hope you never have to face?

3. What trials have you feared in the past that no longer scare you?

4. What can *Helpful Others* do to physically help you during the most difficult trials?

5. Who can you reach out to and encourage when they face similar trials?

Internalization: Help Someone – Go and Teach Someone this Life Tap.

Record your thoughts...
_____
_____
_____

Record what you are grateful for...
_____
_____
_____

Record your commitment to positive action...
_____
_____
_____

Recap: Not everyone wants to see you succeed. Some will even attempt to knock you down. With time, most trials will pass and negative people in life will move on. Prove negative people wrong and overcome your trial.

As a Trial Tapper I find inner strength to adapt and grow stronger from all trials.

CHAPTER 12

TAP #11: Tap Your Hammer – Channel the Pain!

*"Pain and sorrow will trials make,
yet focused efforts will help you overcome and create."*

TAP Overview: This TAP will encourage you to focus your pain on something positive. You will heal faster when you utilize those emotions to produce something productive and tangible. Use your trials to help others.

This visual lesson is titled *Tap Your Hammer*. The image is of a hammer beating down a red-hot piece of steel on an anvil.

This image depicts a blacksmith turning old, ugly metal into something new and beautiful. The hammer can be used to do damage or create new and beautiful creations.

Farmers can take simple metal and create a small sugar maple tap to facilitate the collection of the sap from a tree. This same hammer can be used to hammer in or "tap" into the tree. It takes creativity and time to build functional maple taps. Each year these taps may need repair in order to produce the best outcomes.

Reshaping something ugly into something of beauty is similar to reshaping or reframing your trials and traumas into something useful in the future. As mentioned in the beginning of the book, the reason why you had to endure past trials or traumas may take years to understand. This chapter asks you to find a purpose or cause and to put energy into something positive. As I mentioned previously, internal pain causes energy, and it needs an outlet. Failing to focus this energy into something positive will often cause the energy to become destructive.

I once worked for several months with young adults, ages sixteen to nineteen, who were in foster care. Many were aging out of the foster care system into adulthood. My purpose was to prepare them to take on the responsibilities of adults, and we often talked about the emotional intelligence needed to turn their trials into something positive.

Most of these young adults had many reasons to be angry. They needed to decide how to use their internal energy for something positive. How could they reshape their future? I attempted to help them focus their efforts on positive things that could turn their trials into experiences they could look back on in the future and see growth from.

No matter your trial, there is a strong possibility there are support groups or organizations that are using the painful energy to create something positive that would last. One example would be joining Mothers Against Drunk Drivers (MADD), where surviving family members focus their energies to create support groups and to influence legislation to change laws.

The key, again, is to focus your energy on things you can control in order to turn your trials into strengths. You are the only one who has the key to your freedom and knows how to use the energy for something productive. You need to put your energy into something you find helpful. If you are a surviving family member of a drunk driver, you may not want to focus your energy by joining MADD but instead can find peace in some other endeavor. The challenge is for you to control the energy and use the *Hammer* in a productive, not a destructive, way. This is not a sledgehammer destroying everything in its path. This is a small hammer strategically used to create something positive in your life.

As a child I could not control my parents' divorce. I could not control the abuse. I could not control the poverty I was living in as a teen. The anger and energy inside of me were real, and I did not feel like I had an outlet to discuss my feelings. Like most boys at this age, I did not know how to express my feelings and emotions. I had three big reasons to be angry, and I could have acted out with anger towards others or self-harm with drug use which some of my friends were experimenting with at the time. By the age of fifteen I had plenty of anger, and I decided to take up wrestling my freshman year in high school. This sport helped me channel my energy and anger into something productive. The next four years I was able to help myself and others become successful in this sport.

Although my grades were terrible and I was constantly failing, I decided to focus my energy and efforts on preparing for college to become a social worker. I began working with both victims and perpetrators of sexual abuse. I eventually became responsible for verifying that all federal sex offenders in my state were registered and approving the treatment plans for each of them who were on probation. I had strategically used my energy and *Hammer* to help sexual perpetrators learn how to control their urges in the hopes that it will protect other children from becoming victims in the future.

Shaping an old piece of metal into something useful will take time and effort. Turning your trials into something positive may take years to develop. Realize you have the choice to control the energy inside and shape the outcome or final version of the trial in your favor.

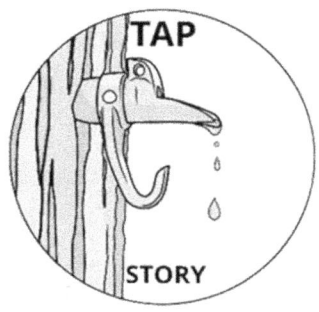

TAP Story: Son's Bus Cards
Main TAP Tool: Hammer
Low Point/Stress Point: Attention all school bus drivers. We have a missing five-year old boy. Does anyone out there have an extra child on their bus? Please respond.

Trial Story: When my oldest son was five years old, my wife and I decided to go on vacation to a remote area with no phone service. My mother-in-law was tasked with watching the children, and every day after school she would take a stroller with my other two children to the bus stop to pick up my five-year-old son.

One day my son did not get off the bus as expected. She frantically asked the bus driver to call to the dispatch office, who in turn asked the other bus drivers if they had an extra boy on their bus. For what seemed to her like an eternity, my son could not be found. Their assumption was that he got on the wrong bus. Finally, one bus driver saw my son walking on the side of a very busy highway and felt prompted to pull her bus over on the side of the road to investigate.

My son would not talk to the strange bus driver; however, she found a postcard in his backpack from us on our trip. Eventually he was reunited with his frantic grandmother. We were unaware of this event until we returned home from our vacation.

Growth Actions: Our family had moved into this new rapidly-growing community. My wife was involved with the school and had already successfully moved a bus stop from one side of the busy highway to another and moved the crosswalk to where there was less traffic. Losing my son in this manner was another opportunity for us to help improve the safety of all children in the neighborhood.

Needless to say, when we returned home from our trip we had a lot of angry energy that needed an outlet. We decided to go to the school and talk to the principal to ask him how he planned to keep this from happening to any more children in the future. The problem was this was a new, overwhelmed principal who had no answers for us. However, he welcomed any suggestions we might have. In an attempt to help find solutions, the next day we went to the school to observe what normally happened when school let out for the day. It was basically chaos as hundreds of children ran to and fro looking for their buses. We even had children coming up to us in tears asking which bus they should get on.

TAP to Strong Growth: Because we were getting no answers from the principal, we needed to come up with our own solutions. After we returned home and calmed down from what we had witnessed, we started brainstorming all the possible ways the bus loading process could be improved. Eventually, it became clear how we could keep our children and others safe in the future. The next day, we made an appointment to meet with the superintendent of the school district. During the meeting we proposed the following: First, send a letter to the parents of all the students in the school district informing them that if a child missed the bus, they could go to the office and use the phone. Second, teachers wearing colorful vests would take turns going out to the buses to help lost students find their buses. Third, buses would be assigned to specific locations to park. Fourth, bus drivers would put visual placards in the windows of their buses. This was the most important recommendation.

Why was this important? Like most school districts at the beginning of the school year, all children riding a bus were given bus numbers to memorize; for example, bus number 872. Our five-year-old, who was having difficulty recognizing numbers and counting, had to memorize a very difficult series of numbers assigned to his bus. Teaching a five-year-old to recognize and remember a three-digit number was hard enough, but if a bus broke down, the principal would make an announcement like this over the intercom: "Bus 872 is being replaced with 694." This was like speaking Chinese to the kindergartners. Our solution was for each bus driver to pick an easily recognizable logo or cartoon character to place in the bus window above those long numbers.

TAP to a Lifetime of Growth: To our amazement, the superintendent implemented the requested changes. Moving forward, the children were assigned a bus logo like the Broncos football team logo or a unicorn or SpongeBob. Then if bus 872 broke down, administrators would move the placard to another bus, and the children would still be able to find the right bus. For years every time I see a school bus, I see a variety of these placards. While writing this book I went to visit the district bus yard. I was received well by the staff and happy to find that for the last eighteen years, buses in this school district and others across the state have used visual placards for all their buses. I had a discussion with the head bus mechanic, who reported they no longer refer to buses by numbers. They prefer the names of the logos. Talk about reframing a negative situation! My son got left behind when he was five, and his children will soon start school riding a bus with placards inspired by their father. Isn't that awesome!

Actual Photos of Bus cards after 18 Years

TRIAL TAPPERS

Iron workers heat up an ugly piece of iron and then mold it into a beautiful work of art by beating it with a hammer. Imagine yourself as the iron worker changing your trial into something better.

1. What specifically do you want to change about your life in relation to this trial?

2. What internal thoughts and personal actions have kept you from turning this trial into a strength?

3. What is the biggest obstacle that stands in the way of you making the change?

4. What will your success look like to others?

5. Who might you ask for help to turn your trial into a strength?

6. What will you do with this new inner strength to help others?

Internalization: Help Someone – Go and Teach Someone this Life Tap.

Record your thoughts...

Record what you are grateful for...

Record your commitment to positive action...

Recap: Focus you pain on something positive. Use your emotions on something productive and tangible. Use your trials to help others.

As a Trial Tapper I replace trauma with hope by changing my trial into a strength.

• CHAPTER 13 •

TAP #12: Tap Your Inner Fire – The Long Process Works!

*"Addressing the fire can make you feel beat,
but the heat can create a future that's sweet."*

TAP Overview: This TAP uses the process of turning maple sap into maple syrup to explain how you can turn pain into strength. It takes a lot of heat and time to produce sweet maple syrup. Each drop of sap taken from the taps of the sugar maple tree can be compared to teardrops from the pain of your trial. Your process to recovery can seem like a trial by fire. Many people have been able to turn pain into strength, and so can you!

This visual lesson is *Tap Your Inner Fire*. The image is of large pots of maple sap hanging over a raging fire.

Turning maple sap into sweet syrup takes fire. When farmers tap maple trees, the trees need to be about forty years old, or the trunks should be at least ten inches across. Once they decide which trees to tap, it generally takes forty gallons of maple sap to make just one gallon of syrup. After collecting the sap, the farmers will need to bring it to a boil. This process usually takes place outside and can take up to fourteen hours over a wood fire heated to 104 degrees Celsius (219 degrees Fahrenheit). This will allow the sap to boil down into syrup.

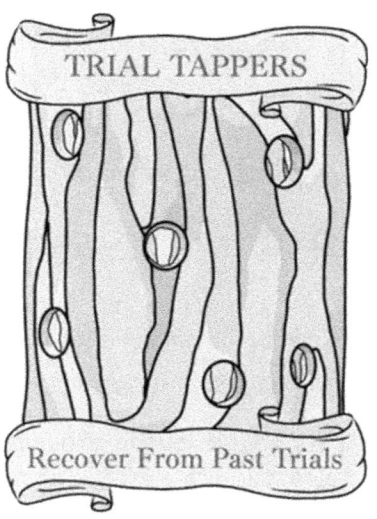

Tapping a tree in this manner usually does not kill the tree. Although drilling a hole in the tree creates a wound, the tree can recover. Its health is not endangered. Farmers are able to tap the same trees for decades without adversely affecting the health of the tree. Most trees will heal or the tap hole will grow over in one year.

This entire book has been about helping you see that you can tap your pain and turn it into something powerful and productive. A maple tree that has been tapped many times over will continue living, yet it will still have the healing marks. You will have different trials than those around you. Past trials are real and will leave marks, but you can recover over time. Surviving the first year of a particular trial is a good way to measure your progress.

Just like the maple sap that is collected, boiled, and changed into something positive, you can endure the pain of the original trial and make the choice to endure additional pain in order to create something positive in the future.

A drop of maple sap can be likened to a teardrop. Just as different trees produce different amounts of sap, some of your trials will produce different amounts of pain. Some life trials only produce minor setbacks or a minor amount of sap; for example, not getting the promotion you wanted at work or having a relationship end suddenly. Other trials will produce major pain and a large amount of sap or tears, such as getting divorced or a having a loved one die unexpectedly.

Across the world we have seen mass shootings or terrorist attacks. These sudden trials and traumas have been very painful for many. A positive movement has been to label the survivors and the community as STRONG. Examples are Paris Strong, Boston Strong, or Vegas Strong. These movements are helpful to many and can be a guide for you in your trials. Some survivors find strength in mourning with others. Some choose to take up a cause or charity. A common theme is for survivors to focus on the strength to move forward and not give away any more power to those who hurt them. They tap their pain and use that energy to create something positive for the future.

Often people who have been diagnosed with diseases such as cancer discover they have become very powerful, hopeful, and appreciative of the small things in life. A close college friend had a severely handicapped brother who could not speak. He required constant attention including feeding, changing, and moving. When I mentioned to her that this must be a very difficult trial for their family, she pleasantly surprised me with her answer, "This was the best thing that ever happened to our family. This has brought us closer to each other and given us a common goal to make his life as comfortable as possible. His innocence makes us want to be a better family so we can all join him in heaven with God someday." From my viewpoint it looked like a major trial, but from hers it was a major blessing. Isn't that awesome?

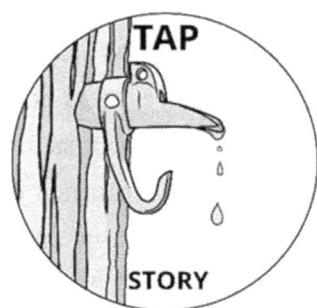

TAP Story: My Trial of Fire

Main TAP Tool: Inner Fire

Low Point/Stress Point: I can't believe what I have been going through the past six months. The death of my brother and facing the man who abused me was too much to keep inside. I have to do something to move forward, but what?

Trial Story: The death of my brother Cody was almost more than I could handle. I feel a special bond to both of my younger brothers, as they lived with us for a summer while my mother and stepfather were attempting to repair their marriage prior to their divorce.

I felt like Cody's part-time parent while his adopted parents were out of state. I attended Cody's school's maturation class about hygiene and the birds and bees. I played catcher for him as he learned to pitch a baseball. I helped him with homework. Eventually my parents' marriage failed, and I was very involved in assisting my mother as she navigated the legal system to seek custody and coordinate visitation. My relationship with Cody came with the added pressure for me, as the oldest child, to guide him in positive directions.

Being confronted by the man who abused me as a child at my brother's viewing was a surreal and extremely unfair situation for me. In my mind, the past abuse had been resolved, and I was sure I would never have to contend with the abuser again.

Growth Actions: I was very involved in helping both my mother and estranged stepfather deal with the search and rescue team looking for my brother. Once Cody was found, I was responsible for informing my siblings and other friends.

The focus was all on Cody as we prepared for his funeral. The surreal experience involving the abuser was unwanted, unexpected, and went unprocessed for several months as I attempted to pass through the *Yoyo Grief Cycle* of my brother's passing. My internal problem began shortly after the funeral.

TAP to Strong Growth: I began having difficulty sleeping and focusing, and feelings of worry and remorse kept showing up without notice. Experiencing months of sleeplessness was a big predictor that I needed professional help. So I started my growth by making attempts to separate and process both the loss of my brother Cody and the loss of my childhood innocence. I decided to go to therapy and face the remaining unresolved traumas and feelings of loss. Reliving all the events and lost moments with Cody during my life was challenging. Reliving all the events and scary moments with the abuse as a child was harder than I thought. I truly had to endure the TAP to Growth I teach to so many of my clients in order to grow stronger. This was a true trial by fire for me.

TAP to a Lifetime of Growth: I found it helpful to begin writing down my feelings and sharing these trials with others in the form of this book. I never wanted to deal with these issues in public, and I hope you never have to experience them for yourselves. My hope is that you who suffer can find joy in your lives and that this book will help you along the path of personal peace.

Your decision to make a positive change after a trial can be difficult, but it is worth it in the end. Your journey in life will be made up of hundreds of growth opportunities due to trials you face.

As stated previously, it takes work, time, persistence, and fire to turn maple sap into sweet syrup. The large pot of sap will endure the final "trial by fire" to reach its potential.

Different faiths talk about trials in life being like a refiner's fire. The sap must boil for a long period of time. Your growth from a trial may also take some time. You can turn your trials into growth opportunities. You are more than one past trial or trauma. You have purpose in this life, and I encourage you to look back at your trials and find strength. You are a survivor and can find others to help you endure any pain or fire. You can identify others who have turned trials into strengths. Your trials have given you, and will continue to give you, new skills, insights, and strength.

Be positive about the future as your recovery and potential growth will continue for years to come. I challenge you to go through the fire and turn it into something positive.

Turning maple tree sap into sweet syrup requires many hours of extreme heat. Imagine that the trials you experience are like this maple sap. Enduring the long trial of fire will make you stronger!

1. How do you define your purpose in life?

2. Visualize a plan to turn your trial of fire into something different. What will it look like?

3. What internal change will you make to move from a victim to survivor?

4. What positive things have you learned about yourself during past trials?

5. List five ways others have changed their personal trials of fire to help others create positive change.

6. What will your success look like in ...

    One year?

    Five years?

    Ten years?

Internalization: Help Someone – Go and Teach Someone this Life Tap.

Record your thoughts…

_____
_____
_____

Record what you are grateful for…

_____
_____
_____

Record your commitment to positive action…

_____
_____
_____

Recap: The process to recovery can seem like a trial by fire. It takes a lot of heat and time to produce sweet maple syrup. Each drop of sap from the taps of the sugar maple tree can be compared to teardrops from the pain of a trial. Many people have been able to turn pain into strength, and so can you!

As a Trial Tapper I turn my fire into something positive.

• CHAPTER 14 •

Summary

You have Trial Action Paths (TAPs) available to help you with all trials.

In your mind's eye, you may now be able to imagine all the illustrations I have presented and recognize how they can help you with any trial. The secret to a happier life is recognizing that all these different TAPs connect and overlap from time to time. Although you may not need all the tools all the time, you know they are available when you need them.

Here is the secret to your success. Everyone's trial paths can be tapped to produce positive growth. You have become a Trial Tapper and will be able to use these paths to replace pain with hope in order to change your life and the lives of those around you.

I used to question if I could change the world with these trial paths. I could do it one person at a time, but I finally came to the realization that I needed to open my mouth and share what I had learned with others. I feel it would be wrong of me to hide what I know works to relieve pain, and I hope you will do the same.

The cool thing is, it didn't just work for me; it works for all kinds of people: those experiencing sadness due to a past trial and those experiencing sadness from a current trial. Using the TAPs in this book has helped thousands of people. I have shared a few of their stories with you in this book. Your story is no different than theirs or mine.

In my parting words, let me remind you why you are prepared to replace your pain with strength.

Because...
You are the expert on your life!
You have value in this world!
You have overcome trials in the past!
You can overcome this trial!
You are strong enough to ask for help from others!
You can take positive action steps to recover!
You have grown from past trials,
and you will grow from any current and future trials!
You are resilient!

You might doubt yourself and think I ask too much from you. I have deliberately asked you to write your answers to questions designed to help you understand that there is hope for you. You may think I asked too many questions. However, your thoughts have probably included many reasons why you can't turn your sadness into hope. If you can't see the possibility of hope in your own life, you may be telling yourself there is no way you can help others, right?

I can't begin to list all the false beliefs or questions that may keep you from finding hope and growth from trials. However, the following false beliefs are some examples of what you might be thinking. I have followed them up with true statements that contradict those false beliefs.

There is no way out of my sadness. I have tried everything. Everyone will experience trials from time to time. If you asked ten people you know if they are experiencing a trial, my guess is more than half will answer yes. Just because you did not find the right person or tools to help in the past does not mean you won't find them with the help of someone else soon.

No one else understands my particular trial. Your trial is unique to you, but everyone experiences sadness from trials and can relate to your struggle. There is a great chance that there are support groups of others who have experienced a trial very similar to yours.

No one is willing to help me. It's impossible for you to count how many people there are who are willing to listen and help you with your trial, such as friends, volunteers, and professionals.

I can't help anyone with my story. Sharing your story with others strengthens both you and those you tell. My sons agreed to allow me to share their trials. They did this hoping to help other others with similar struggles. They feel that if they help just one person, it's worth it. I have found my strength to tell you my story of my brother's suicide and my childhood abuse. I know sharing my story has helped and is presently helping others.

My life has been a string of failures. I won't succeed as a Trial Tapper. Your failures are what will make you a success. You're still here, and the fact that you have completed this book is proof you can succeed at great things. Through the *Life Growth Timeline*, you have identified past successes, such as graduating high school or securing a job. I purposely listed my failures in this book because these failures have turned me into a Trial Tapper for life!

I'm too shy to talk to others. Sharing your story with others strengthens you and those you tell. It took a lot of practice, but I have gone from being unable to look people in the eye when speaking to standing in front of hundreds to tell my story. If I can do it, you can too. Start by sharing your story and the answers you wrote in this book with those closest to you. Go and teach them what you learned.

I can never learn anything from my trial. Time has a way of healing all wounds. It might be difficult for you to see how you could learn anything from your trial now, but years from now you will. As outlined in this book, I lost my innocence as a child. Now, as an adult, I help thousands.

My *Unseen Power* has forgotten me. Trials come to each of us despite our connections with an *Unseen Power*, and life's storms affect people both good and bad. Millions of people experiencing trials find strength and hope when they seek a closer connection with an *Unseen Power*. Sometimes the joy only comes after they turn the pain and sadness over to an *Unseen Power*. I also struggled with a religious conflict during my childhood while looking for safety. I eventually found strength and peace with my *Unseen Power*.

I have failed in the past. It's hopeless to try. We all fail from time to time in this experience we call life. No one wins every sports game, no one gets every promotion, and few marry their first love. Failure strengthens us. The former Prime Minister of Great Britain, Winston Churchill, said it best: "If you're going through hell, keep going. Attitude is a little thing that makes a BIG difference. Success is not final, failure is not fatal: it is the courage to continue that counts. Never, never, never give up."[5]

I have always been sad, and there is no hope in my life. When you are afraid, no one can tell you not to worry and not to be afraid. I can't tell you to have hope or to be strong and it will all work out. I can't give you hope. The path to find it is yours and yours alone. The truth is that hope, growth, and possibly understanding might be just around the corner. If you can have just a small desire to look for the hope, I know you can find it.

You have Safety and Ground Supports. You need to know that you are not alone in this world, and that others have faced similar trials as identified in the chapter on *Life's Trials*. You know how to identify your *Season of Symptoms*. You know how to prepare for your *Unexpected Storms* in life. You know how to use *Resilient Growth Actions* from past trials. You know how to identify both good and bad with the *Life Growth Timeline*. You know how to keep your *Protective Vest* balanced and strong to endure future trials. You know how to identify *Helpful Others* who are willing to help you succeed. You know that emotional growth moves in patterns, and you can endure TAP to Growth.

---

[5] 50 Sir Winston Churchill Quotes to Live By; http://www.bbcamerica.com/anglophenia/2015/04/50-churchill-quotes

You have Resilience and Education. You know how to recognize *Yoyo Grief Cycles*. You know how to avoid *Pits of Despair* and pitfalls in the future. You know how to use the outside *Resistance* of those around you as a source of strength and motivation.

You have Strengths and Empowerment. You know the effects of trauma and how to empty the trash (*Trauma Trash Can*). You know how to identify where you find strength from *Unseen Power*. You know you might be able to turn your trial into something useful in the future (*Hammer*). You know as you endure the challenging fire you can create great things in the future (*Fire*).

Be grateful for the journey. In every chapter I asked you to identify something you were grateful for in life. I am not asking you to be grateful for your worst trials as I will never be able to say that about the abuse or my brother's suicide. I am trying to help you find hope even during your worst trials as you make attempts to find gratitude for the little things in life. Find something! Go back and read over all the things you identified you were grateful for as you read this book. If you're really struggling, make attempts to write something down each day and place them in a jar or bucket. Pull them out and read them over during your low points or at the end of a week, month, and possibly year. You can start with the things you wrote while reading this book. You should have written down twelve things you are grateful for in life.

This next image is looking down on a collection bucket hanging on a Tap of a tree. The bucket is full of sap water. Floating on the top of the water are twelve stars waiting for you to identify what you are grateful for in life. Write them all down in this grateful bucket.

I give the first two generic examples of being grateful for nature and water.

Face your trials by using the tools outlined in this book to help yourself and others. I commend you for your courage as you continue this journey of growth.

I have shared many of my challenges and those of others I know. I again state that I am no one special. Despite any successes I have had over the years, I will continue to struggle with trials in my future. I have shared the tools that helped me, and I hope you can use some of these tools from time to time to help yourself or others. If my story helps just one person like you find the courage to grow stronger after trials, it will be worth it. I challenge you to go and share what you have learned with others.

It can be startling to have someone point out to you something that has been right in front of you all the time. Sometimes you just need someone with a little more experience to bring it to your attention. Can you see yourself using one of these TAPs with your next trial? Now that you understand the TAP viewpoint and have the skills that can help you overcome any trial, you might be saying to yourself: "It's so simple! How did I not see this before? Of course! I'm seeing new TAPs all around me. Now I have a roadmap or plan for future trials. I have grown. I need to tell others!"

Life happens. You don't ask for trials, and TAPs help prepare you for them when they come. You're just one TAP away…

I hope by now you feel comfortable in identifying yourself as a Trial Tapper. Let me repeat once again the positive statements of a Trial Tapper. I encourage you to read the following out loud. Hear yourself and find your power to survive any trial.

The Trial Tapper's Creed

As a Trial Tapper I recognize that I am not alone in experiencing trials in life.
As a Trial Tapper I see new trials and TAPs as chances to grow.
As a Trial Tapper I admit when I'm sad and going through trials.
As a Trial Tapper I humble myself to accept help from others, including therapists and doctors, during the most difficult traumas.
As a Trial Tapper I draw on Unseen Power to help me overcome any trial.
As a Trial Tapper I prepare for the Unexpected Storms in my future.

As a Trial Tapper I identify those areas in my life that help protect me during trials.

As a Trial Tapper I believe no matter how painful the trial, I can accept a new reality and recover.

As a Trial Tapper I recognize past attempts at growth as positive.

As a Trial Tapper I believe no matter how painful the trauma, I can survive and thrive in the future.

As a Trial Tapper I find inner strength to adapt and grow stronger from all trials.

As a Trial Tapper I replace trauma with hope by changing my trial into a strength.

As a Trial Tapper I turn my fire into something positive.

As a Trial Tapper I can identify my successes with past trials and know that I am the expert on my paths toward growth.

As a Trial Tapper I create personal TAPs to share with the world.

I am a Trial Tapper.

Do You Believe It?

This book is full of the best ideas I have learned from over the years. This book has many examples of others who have grown by doing the steps to answer these questions and teach others. Ultimately, you will have to take the steps to demonstrate your strength to yourself and others.

This book is a combination of stories from my life and those I know who also use TAPs to grow. I know you have meaningful stories. Come up with your own stories that explain how you overcame trials. I challenge you to tell your story to others.

Learn and grow from your trials and move forward. I'll repeat what I often tell people experiencing a trial: "I don't know why this happened. I don't know why you're going through this at this time. And I don't know what you can learn from this experience." You might not understand why you had a particular trial for five, ten, twenty, thirty years, or in my case forty years. I went through a trial I never wanted nor expected, but I'm able to come out on the other end and tell you this story now. I have shared my life's experiences and some of those of a thousand others I worked with over the years. I challenge you to take the final step to create your own story or TAP and compose your questions to teach others. I hope you can find meaning and a purpose in life despite your trials.

One Last Thing: My Life CRP Card

I wish my brother Cody would have realized how many people cared about him. If he were here today, I would ask him some of the same questions that prevented others from committing suicide. I would ask him to tell me about the events of the day that lead up to his decision. I would ask him to tell me what thoughts, emotions, and physical sensations he was having. I would ask him about all the challenges he has had in his life. I would ask him to explain what he wants to be different in his life. I would ask him to find something he was grateful for in life.

I would then give him hope and support, explaining how these challenges are just a moment in time in comparison to his life. I would teach him these TAPs. I would explain to him what the National Center for Veterans Studies has found to be helpful in surviving low points and preventing suicide. He could have used this tool to help him survive.

You can use this simple approach called a Crisis Response Plan (CRP) by David C. Rozek, PhD. This is not a suicide contract, but a tangible visible memory aid to help you identify when you're in an emotional crisis and provide you with strategies to help you recover and get help.

You know best what has helped and what will help you during your weakest points in life. Prepare now to identify those warning signs and create a plan for how you will get help. You can do this with a 5x7-inch flash card. You identify personal warning signs, self-management helps, reasons for living, and helpful or supportive others. You identify steps to take in a crisis.

Consider the following when your life is in crisis:

1. What are some of the things you notice inside yourself?

2. What are some situations or indicators that things are not going so well for you? What are your warning signs?

3. How might others know when you're in trouble? What is observable or visible?

4. What are your reasons for living and what gives you sense of purpose and meaning in life?

5. Ultimately, what stands in the way of you hurting yourself?

6. Who can you identify who will help and support you during a crisis?

7. Which family or friends can your call?

8. What helps calm you down or make you feel less stressed?

9. What things have you found to be helpful in the past, even if you don't do those things anymore?

10. Who would you call in an emergency when all else has failed to keep you from considering suicide?

11. Who are your support services in an extreme emergency? Your therapist or doctor?

12. Identify those to call or places to go for immediate help, such as suicide hotlines, 911, or your local hospital, fire or police stations.

There is a National Suicide Prevention Lifeline at 1-800-273-TALK [8255].

If you go to the Internet you will find many helpful resources. I love using a smart phone app called *Virtual Hope Box*.

This app has many things to distract, relax, cope, and inspire. You can also upload your own photos.

Commit to filling out this card and placing a photo of your family or pet on the back. Take a photo of the card with your phone and give a copy to family or friends so they will know what to do to best help you.

I have placed an example of my Life CRP Card in this book and left a blank one for you to fill out for yourself.

I Walked With You

Cody,

As your oldest brother I have walked with you on your journey in this life.

I walked with you as you learned to walk and run.

I walked with you on my wedding day as you walked down the aisle before my bride.

I walked with you as you and your brother lived with my wife and children.

I walked with you as we built your baseball mound and plate to teach you how to pitch.

I walked with you as I made you mow the neighbors' yards as your punishment for acting out.

I walked with you for parent-teacher conference to talk about your grades.

I nervously walked with you to Boys Maturation class to learn about the birds and the bees.

I fought for you as our parents decided to divorce and became unreasonable towards each other.

I laughed with you as we spent vacation time together over the years. I rejoiced with you as you brought children into this world and how proud you were to be a father.

I always thought of you even when we drifted apart and walked different paths.

I celebrated you as you succeeded in your career making people happy. I prayed for you as you struggled with your pains in life.

I was happy for you when mom would tell me stories of your time together.

I staggered toward you as I approached your casket to say goodbye.

I find hope knowing we will walk and laugh together again in heaven.

I Love You.

Big Brother Hugh

For all those who suffer, I give you this gift of a Life CRP Card.

Please take a 5x7 "flash card" and answer the following questions for yourself.

Keep this card in your wallet for those trials that seem too difficult to handle. Give out duplicate copies of this card to those close to you.

I just wish Cody would have had one of these on him the day he gave up on life.

Take a moment and fill out your own CRP card.

CRP Card Questions:

1. What observable or visible behaviors would you demonstrate if you were at the point of despair? Examples: crying, hitting things, can't get out of bed

2. List things that calm you and give you hope. Examples: breathing for ten minutes, going for a walk, listening to calm music

3. What are some reasons to live? Examples: wife, children, friends

4. Who can you call if these things don't work?

    1. Best friend
    2. Therapist Phone #
    3. Hotline 1-800-273-2755
    4. Hospital or 911

It would look like this:

Warning Signs
1. Crying 2. Getting Angry 3. Not Talking 4. Sick

Reasons for Living
1. Wife 2. Children 3. Grandchildren 4. Friends 5. Religious Reasons

Support
1. Wife 2. Jason 3. Rick 4. Greg 5. Religious Leader

What Helps?
1. Breathing 10. Min. 2. Meditation 3. Garden
4. Home Depot 5. Playing with Grandkids
6. Online videos 7. Self-help books 8. Volunteer 9. Pray

Emergency – Need Help Now
1. Call a Therapist 2. Call Dr. 3. Call Hotline 1-800-273-2755
4. Go to Fire station 5. Go to Hospital 6. Call 911

My Life CRP Card

Warning Signs				
1.	2.	3.	4.	5.
Reasons for Living				
1.	2.	3.	4.	5.
Support				
1.	2.	3.	4.	5.
What Helps?				
1.	2.	3.	4.	5.
6.	7.	8.	9.	10.
Emergency – Need Help Now				
1. Call a Therapist	2. Call Dr.		3. Call Hotline 1-800-273-2755	
4. Go to Fire station	5. Go to Hospital		6. Call 911	

Your Life CRP Card

References and Works Cited

SAMHSA's *Six Key Principles of a Trauma-Informed Approach Trauma-specific Interventions*, website: www.samhsa 2019

Centers for Disease Control and Prevention, Kaiser Permanente. *The ACE Study Survey Data* [Unpublished Data]. Atlanta, Georgia: U.S. Department of Health and Human Services, Centers for Disease Control and Prevention; 2016. Source http://www.integration.samhsa.gov/clinical-practice/trauma 2019

Crisis Response Plan, National Center for Veterans Studies, the University of Utah, David C. Rozek, PhD

Kubler-Ross model, *Five Stages of Grief*, Book titled *On Death and Dying* 1969.

National Domestic Violence Hotline, *50 Obstacles to Leaving: 1-10*; June 10, 2013

National Alliance on Mental Illness (NAMI) Reports

- Any Mental Illness (AMI) Among Adults. (n.d.). Retrieved May 1, 2019, from https://www.nimh.nih.gov/health/statistics/mental-illness.shtml#part_154785
- Serious Mental Illness (SMI) Among Adults. (n.d.). Retrieved May 1, 2019, from https://www.nimh.nih.gov/health/statistics/mental-illness.shtml#part_154788
- Major Depression Among Adults. (n.d.). Retrieved January 16, 2015, from

http://www.nimh.nih.gov/health/statistics/prevalence/major-depression-among-adults.shtml
- Any Anxiety Disorder Among Adults. (n.d.). Retrieved January 16, 2015, from http://www.nimh.nih.gov/health/statistics/prevalence/any-anxiety-disorder-among-adults.shtml
- Substance Abuse and Mental Health Services Administration, *Results from the 2014 National Survey on Drug Use and Health: Mental Health Findings*, NSDUH Series H-50, HHS Publication No. (SMA) 15-4927. Rockville, MD: Substance Abuse and Mental Health Services Administration. (2015). Retrieved October 27, 2015

TRIAL TAPPERS

Would You Provide a Testimonial?

I hope you now call yourself a Trial Tapper and want to share your new insights with others. The success of this book depends on constant sharing and, most importantly, reviews on the Internet. Why? You have no idea how important sharing just one sentence about this book helps others decide to purchase. Please spread the word by writing a quick review on Amazon or Goodreads and post about it on your Internet social media sites. Every review makes a HUGE difference. I ask you to take a few minutes now and share your growth with others! Here are some questions to help you with your review or post. Thank you.

1. Why did you enjoy *Trial Tappers*?

2. In a sentence or two, what would you say to another about *Trial Tappers* and what it's done for you?

3. What is your single greatest take away from the *Trial Tappers*?

4. What was your problem before you bought *Trial Tappers*?

5. What results have you received from *Trial Tappers*?

6. What exactly did you like most about *Trial Tappers*?

7. Why would you recommend *Trial Tappers* to others?

8. What, specifically, was your favorite part of *Trial Tappers* and why?

9. If you were to recommend *Trial Tappers* to your best friend, what would you say?

10. What are three benefits you've experienced as a result of the *Trial Tappers*?

11. Would you recommend *Trial Tappers*? If so, why?

12. What was life like before you started reading *Trial Tappers*?

13. What is life like now that you've finished reading *Trial Tappers*?

14. What surprised you the most or made you the happiest about *Trial Tappers*?

15. Do you have any other benefits you want to mention about *Trial Tappers*, or is there anything else you want to add?

Thanks for your input! Do I have permission to use your comments as a testimonial for *Trial Tappers* and Hugh Watt in future marketing efforts?

If you liked this book, I encourage you to obtain the companion sets of cards to help you remember the lessons. These cards can be found on my website or at www.thegamecrafter.com. I also encourage you to obtain my ebooks, paperbacks, or audiobooks of this and my second book *Trial Tappers: Harvesting More of Life's Trials to Produce Positive Growth.*

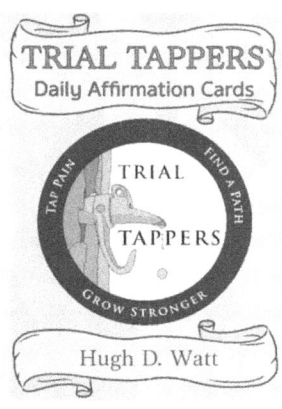

ABOUT THE AUTHOR

Hugh decided to write this self-help book after his younger brother decided to commit suicide and he came face-to-face with the man who sexually abused him as a child during the funeral service. As a licensed clinician, he has unique insight into the worst trials and traumas people experience in life. He simplifies learning in a way that has allowed him to successfully help others to understand that trials and trauma in life can produce growth.

Hugh has helped thousands of people grow resilient after trials in their lives. This book will give you tools in the form of visual stories with questions that will help guide you to overcome all types of trials from health and finance or traumas from sex abuse to suicide in your life.

This book will show you how to symbolically use the process of collecting maple tree sap as a way to overcome your trials. A sugar maple tree needs to be tapped in order to collect sweet sap, which is hidden inside the tree. This sap is then processed into maple syrup. Much like the process it takes to actively drill into a maple tree to get to the sap, a Trial Tapper is someone who recognizes that answers and growth come from within a person when they choose to take one of several proven paths after any trial. Over time, a Trial Tapper grows stronger and wants to share those positive paths with the world.

Trial Tappers take positive steps away from being a victim and towards being a survivor. We can use positive actions and choose to take one of several proven paths to become stronger after any trial. A Trial Tapper will use one of the TAPs in this book to move away from pain and towards hope.

Hugh uses his own personal trials and those of others he knows to demonstrate that resilience is possible after any trial. He has worked with both teens and adults who were experiencing all types of personal storms, including sexual and physical abuse, addictions, domestic violence, incarceration, anxiety, depression, bullying, suicide, family problems, terminal illness, financial struggles, and loss, to name a few.

Hugh earned a Master's Degree from the University of Denver in Social Work and is a Licensed Clinical Social Worker (LCSW). He became the Clinical Director of the 400-bed residential substance abuse program called Con-Quest, the largest residential program in the State of Utah. Prior to leaving this position, he received the prestigious Director's Award from the Utah Department of Corrections for transforming a struggling program into a Therapeutic Community program with less than 30 percent recidivism.

Hugh then began working as a U.S. Probation Officer and approves and coordinates sex offender, mental health, and substance abuse treatment for all federal felons releasing from prison in his state. He is a former University of Utah board member having served on the Institutional Review Board (IRB). His more than twenty years of clinical experience has required him to complete both the State of Utah Corrections and Federal Law Enforcement Training (FLETC) academies. While working as a U.S. Probation Officer, he was a founding member of the federal drug court program called Reentry Independence through Sustainable Efforts (RISE) and a former Co-Chair to the U.S. Chief District Court Judge, Assisting Reentry to our Communities (ARC) program. He has been certified as a Critical Incident Stress Management (CISM) team member for law enforcement. Hugh has presented to many large groups to include the Correctional Education Association Leadership Forum and the National Forensic Counselors Association. He has been married for more than 26 years and has three sons.

www.ingramcontent.com/pod-product-compliance
Lightning Source LLC
Chambersburg PA
CBHW061428040426
42450CB00007B/953